Project Management Institute

NAVIGATING COMPLEXITY:
A PRACTICE GUIDE

Library of Congress Cataloging-in-Publication Data

Navigating complexity : a practice guide / Project Management Institute.
      pages cm
   Includes bibliographical references.
   ISBN-13: 978-1-62825-036-7 (alk. paper)
   ISBN-10: 1-62825-036-4 (alk. paper)
   1. Leadership. 2. Communication in management. 3. Critical thinking. 4. Strategic planning. I. Project Management
Institute.
   HD57.7.N385 2014
   658.4'04--dc23

                                          2013049393

ISBN: 978-1-62825-036-7

Published by:
      Project Management Institute, Inc.
      14 Campus Boulevard
      Newtown Square, Pennsylvania 19073-3299 USA
      Phone: +610-356-4600
      Fax: +610-356-4647
      Email: customercare@pmi.org
      Internet: www.PMI.org

PMI Publications welcomes corrections and comments on its books. Please feel free to send comments on typographical,
formatting, or other errors. Simply make a copy of the relevant page of the book, mark the error, and send it to: Book Editor, PMI
Publications, 14 Campus Boulevard, Newtown Square, PA 19073-3299 USA.

To inquire about discounts for resale or educational purposes, please contact the PMI Book Service Center.
      PMI Book Service Center
      P.O. Box 932683, Atlanta, GA 31193-2683 USA
      Phone: 1-866-276-4764 (within the U.S. or Canada) or +1-770-280-4129 (globally)
      Fax: +1-770-280-4113
      Email: info@bookorders.pmi.org

The paper used in this book complies with the Permanent Paper Standard issued by the National Information Standards
Organization (Z39.48—1984).

10 9 8 7 6 5 4 3 2 1

NOTICE

TABLE OF CONTENTS

LIST OF TABLES AND FIGURES

PREFACE

Navigating Complexity: A Practice Guide is a complementary document to PMI's foundational standards. This practice guide provides guidance to organizations and practitioners on how to manage programs and projects that are impacted by complexity. This practice guide exemplifies PMI's continuing commitment to support the project management profession with a defined body of knowledge.

While complexity varies depending on an individual's perspective, experience, and knowledge, complexity may be viewed as challenging characteristics of programs and projects that organizations and practitioners encounter in today's fast-paced, competitive, dynamic environment. In order to navigate complexity, efforts such as setting up the appropriate organizational structure, diligently researching the program or project prior to approval, cultivating talents, fostering leadership, practicing effective communications, nurturing flexibility, being resilient, and applying critical thinking to implement appropriate, thoughtful action plans are necessary.

A Guide to the Project Management Body of Knowledge (PMBOK® Guide), *The Standard for Program Management*, *The Standard for Portfolio Management*, and *Organizational Project Management Maturity Model (OPM3®)* provide the foundational concepts, processes, tools, and techniques for the profession. These foundations are applicable and useful as part of the resources in navigating complexity. The ability to appropriately choose and tailor an approach, tool, or technique may come with experience but preparedness, awareness, and vigilance should elevate the chances for successful outcomes.

A practice guide is a new category in the PMI library of standards, which is intended to encourage discussion related to areas of practice where there may not yet be consensus. Innovation, combined with a dynamic external environment, drives the need for organizations and practitioners to act more decisively and become more adaptive to navigate complexity. PMI introduced this practice guide to identify useful approaches for integration with PMI's foundational standards.

Practice guides are developed by leading experts in the field using a new process that provides reliable information and reduces the time required for development and distribution. PMI defines a practice guide as a standards product that provides supporting supplemental information and instructions for the application of PMI standards. Practice guides are not full consensus-based standards and do not go through the exposure draft process. However, the resulting work may be introduced later as a potential standard and, if so, will then be subjected to PMI's documented process for the development of full consensus standards.

1

INTRODUCTION

Since the advent of Project Management Institute's (PMI) *A Guide to the Project Management Body of Knowledge"* (*PMBOK® Guide*) [1][1] in early 1983, the number of practitioners[2] has increased significantly as well as the range and level of complexities of programs and projects. For the purpose of this practice guide, complexity is a characteristic of a program or project or its environment that is difficult to manage due to human behavior, system behavior, and ambiguity. Complexity is not directly proportional to the size of a program or project; small programs and projects may contain substantial complexity. In any program and project with complexity, there are inherent risks and uncertainties that need to be addressed.

Complexity in programs and projects has always existed (e.g., building of the pyramids, geographical infrastructure development, government or military procurement projects, and various national or international space programs). However, globalization, new technologies, and fragmented supply chains have significantly increased and compounded the complexity of what practitioners are being asked to manage. Because organizational leaders are expecting more complexity in the years to come and because there are more budgets at risk for programs and projects with complexity [2], there is an urgent need for successful delivery of such programs and projects, especially those with elements of complexity. As a result, there have been a variety of studies and publications on complexity; but few focus on providing practitioners and organizations with practical approaches to navigate complexity.

This practice guide is intended to provide practitioners and organizations with practical ways to recognize and navigate complexity. The presence of complexity does not change the foundational program or project management methodology. For example, the method for calculating earned value would be the same. The presence of complexity requires practitioners to focus more on emergent issues, to apply critical thinking, and to know when to give special importance to a specific program or project management processes and Knowledge Areas. While the ability to demonstrate leadership, to effectively communicate, or to tailor a process or select an appropriate tool or approach may need to be cultivated and honed, focus on and awareness of complexity will enhance the likelihood of success in navigating complexity.

This practice guide has been developed for program and project managers at all levels of experience, senior management, and organizations. It is an expansion of and companion to information provided in PMI's four foundational standards including the latest edition of *A Guide to the Project Management Body of Knowledge* (*PMBOK® Guide*), *The Standard for Program Management* [3], *The Standard for Portfolio Management* [4], and *Organizational Project Management Maturity Model* (*OPM3®*) [5], in addition to the *PMI Lexicon of Project Management Terms* [6].

---

[1] The numbers in brackets refer to the list of references at the end of this practice guide.

[2] Throughout this practice guide, the term "practitioner" refers to both program and project manager.

1.1 Purpose and Structure of this Complexity Practice Guide

The purpose of this practice guide is to help practitioners and organizations navigate complexity by providing the following:

- Essential organizational considerations when dealing with complexity to realize portfolio strategic initiatives,

- A practical view of how complexity can be categorized and causes of complexity understood,

- An easy to use complexity assessment, and

- Useful practices, complexity scenarios, and guidance to transform insights into actions and manage the effects of complexity through an action plan.

Drawing on both relevant literature and views of experienced practitioners, this practice guide provides a means to assess and navigate complexity in programs and projects through content presented in the six subsequent sections:

- **Section 2 Organizational Considerations.** Proposes the need for organizational support structures to align people, programs, and projects.

- **Section 3 Encountering Complexity.** Presents the three main categories of complexity: human behavior, system behavior, and ambiguity and their underlying conditions, which represent causes of complexity that contribute to difficulty in managing a program or project.

- **Section 4 PMI Foundational Standards and Useful Practices.** Identifies the four areas (scope, communications, stakeholders, and risk), which present the most challenges when faced with complexity on a program or project, and provides suggested practices that can be employed to address these challenges.

- **Section 5 Navigating Complexity: The Assessment Questionnaire.** Offers a questionnaire to assess and determine potential contributors to complexity in programs and projects.

- **Section 6 Complexity Scenarios and Possible Actions.** Provides situational examples in the form of scenarios that demonstrate complexity associated with a program or project. Possible actions are suggested to help navigate complexity in those situations.

- **Section 7 Developing the Action Plan.** Presents considerations for creating a plan based on actions selected, and the need to monitor and reassess complexity on a program or project on a periodic basis.

While there are numerous elements associated with complexity, this practice guide addresses those elements that are commonly associated with programs and projects.

2

ORGANIZATIONAL CONSIDERATIONS

In today's complex world, organizational preparation is necessary to facilitate the successful execution of programs and projects. This section provides senior management with information on how to enable successful outcomes for programs and projects with complexity, which is important to meeting organizational goals and objectives. Practitioners may also find this section helpful as organizational preparedness will have a significant impact on the execution of their programs and projects regardless of the level of complexity.

In some organizations, senior management may serve in the role of sponsor for programs and projects that contain complexity. Senior management may also be part of the organization's portfolio, program, or project management office (PMO).

According to PMI's *Pulse of the Profession™ In Depth Report: Navigating Complexity* [2], high-performing organizations recognize that, regardless of the degree of complexity, standardized project management practices, effective communications, and a strong talent base are necessary for program and project success. In addition, executives with strong leadership skills play a key role in enabling successful program and project outcomes.

This section addresses some key organizational enablers that can impact the outcome of programs and projects with complexity. Specifically, the following considerations will be addressed:

- Leadership,
- Portfolio management,
- Collaboration for successful outcomes,
- Performance metrics,
- Impact of organizational structures,
- Resource gap analysis, and
- Senior management, practitioner, and team competency.

2.1 Leadership

One of the most important ingredients for the successful navigation of complexity in programs and projects is leadership. Leadership of programs and projects with complexity may require, but is not limited to, the following practices:

- Provide active executive sponsorship and commitment.
- Highlight the critical success of key programs and projects to the organization.
- Empower the program and project manager and provide the program or project team with the organizational support to facilitate successful delivery of results and benefits.
- Be aware of early warning signs of problems and put action plans in place to address, as needed.
- Use a flexible leadership style, which implies that the style changes with the situation and the program or project team or individuals.

For programs and projects with complexity, it is recommended that senior management communicate the importance of critical programs and projects to the entire enterprise so as to reinforce the organization's commitment to a program or project. One effective method employed by senior management is to prioritize programs and projects and communicate that prioritization to the impacted organizations. When senior management highlights that a certain program or project is of a higher priority for meeting organizational goals and objectives, then the team is more likely to receive the necessary support from other operational functions.

Flexible leadership is about being able to adapt leadership style to changing situations and stakeholders. Depending on the situation, a flexible leader may use various approaches tailored to the situation.

2.2 Portfolio Management

One element of complexity that can impact an approved or selected program or project is a shift in organizational strategy, which may require portfolio management realignment. In some cases, the organization (a) may decide that the program or project is no longer of strategic value and may cancel the program or project; or (b) may request that the scope and objectives of the program or project be revised to align with new organizational strategy. Portfolio management provides an organization with the means to successfully manage change in strategy. Additional information on this topic can be found in *Managing Change in Organizations: A Practice Guide* [7].

According to *The Standard for Portfolio Management,* portfolio management enables the organization to leverage program or project selection and facilitate successful execution. In addition, portfolio management supports a strong and profitable organization within a competitive and rapidly changing environment. The portfolio should be monitored closely so as to determine precise statuses and trends.

Portfolio management is a key driver for navigating complexity. The PMI *Pulse of Profession™ In-Depth Report: Portfolio Management* [8] reports the following essential practices used by organizations that are highly effective in portfolio management:

- **Elevate portfolio management to a strategic level.** Senior management understands and supports the practice of portfolio management.
- **Create a portfolio-minded culture.** Senior management is willing to show their support of portfolio management through communication, investment, dedicated resources, and education.
- **Implement appropriate tools and practices.** Senior management understands the need to implement appropriate formal portfolio management tools and practices and to standardize portfolio management.

2.3 Collaboration for Successful Outcomes

Collaboration between senior management and the program or project manager is an important enabler for the successful outcome of programs or projects with a high degree of complexity.

Some collaborative factors that provide successful outcomes for programs or projects with complexity include:

- Ongoing communication between the program or project sponsor and the program or project manager;
- Intrinsic and extrinsic rewards that are tailored to individual and group motivations;
- Utilization of change management practices to better adapt to new emerging situations and conditions;
- Easy and prompt accessibility of senior management to the program or project manager; and
- Investment and support of interdepartmental, cross-professional collaboration and multidisciplinary project team integration.

The collaboration between the sponsor and the program or project manager provides for transparency, increased communication, and effective decision making. The need for this collaboration becomes apparent during the program or project when encountering such items as emerging requirements, impediments, issues, and risks. These items encountered during the program or project can negatively impact the program or project's progress when collaboration is absent.

2.4 Performance Metrics

Organizations need information throughout the program or project life cycle in order to understand its current health and to be able to predict success. Metrics can support the effective communication and reinforce awareness of the project or program purpose with stakeholders. Metrics vary across industries and types of programs and projects. Successful organizations tend to have multiple key performance indicators (KPIs) perspectives on a program or project throughout its life cycle. Some organizations have both preproject KPIs, multiple perspectives during implementation, and measurements of success after the program or project finishes. Successful organizations also include portfolio-level KPIs across programs and projects.

Organizations may look at metrics that are not specific to programs or projects, such as business drivers that may include resource retention and utilization. These metrics are used to help assess the success of the program or project and the overall portfolio.

Metrics can be derived for several performance categories; the following provides some category examples:

- Schedule,
- Financial,
- Earned value,
- Scope,
- Quality,

- Changes,
- Customer satisfaction,
- Process,
- Risk,
- Resources, and
- Procurement.

A robust set of metrics can provide insights into the program or project and help predict program and project success [9].

2.5 Impact of Organizational Structures

It is important for senior management to have a full understanding of the impact that organizational structures can have on the successful execution of programs and projects with complexity. Structure should fit the needs of the dynamic organizational environment and align with strategy.

Within program and project management, there are three types of organizational structures that are noted in the *PMBOK® Guide:* projectized, matrix, and functional. When dealing with complexity, a modified structure may be necessary. For example, a flatter or leaner organizational structure may allow for faster or more creative decision making. Senior management should provide the appropriate level of decision-making authority. With the delegated authority, the program or project managers should be held accountable for results.

The most useful organizational structure depends on multiple facets of the program or project, along with industry considerations and enterprise environmental factors. In order to increase the likelihood of success, an organizational structure may require flexibility and adjustment, thereby enabling the attainment of organizational goals and objectives.

2.5.1 Leveraging PMO Support and Governance

A portfolio, program, or project management office (PMO) is an organizational structure that may be used to standardize the portfolio, program, or project-related governance processes and facilitate the sharing of resources, methodologies, tools, and techniques. Some organizations find that having an enterprise (or organization-wide) portfolio, program, or project management office, sometimes called a center of excellence, is an effective integrating function because it has visibility of and influence on all related portfolio, program, or project management activities. An enterprise PMO may be structured and leveraged in many ways to address and successfully overcome complexity, such as through ongoing support and governance. A few examples of the benefits that enterprise PMOs can provide to practitioners include, but are not limited to the following:

- Provide structure through standardized processes, procedures, and guidelines, which allows practitioners to better navigate through complexity.

2

- Provide guidance on how to perform program or project assessments and define when and how they are to be used.

- Institute gate reviews and audits, which lead to better control and decision making.

- Specify roles and responsibilities, which allow for greater clarity and reduce ambiguity.

- Provide governance through standardized tools and templates, and support through expert feedback, mentoring, and guidance in order to eliminate roadblocks.

- Maintain organizational process assets, such as historical databases and lessons learned, which may reduce the unknown, thereby potentially reducing the effects of complexity.

- Provide or require training on managing program or project complexity.

In collaboration with the practitioner, the enterprise PMO provides effective support and resources to identify early warning signs of unanticipated changes and anomalies that may suggest the potential for system difficulty or even failure.

The enterprise PMO team should clearly communicate and provide value to the organization. An enterprise PMO team should help break down information silos that exist (or are perceived to exist). However, when not carefully structured or administered, an enterprise PMO may add to the level of complexity. It is important for enterprise PMOs to ensure that organizational procedures do not limit the flexibility of the program or project team. An enterprise PMO should maintain flexibility within standardized processes, procedures, and guidelines, to ensure that these can be tailored to address the level of complexity that exists, or may arise, within a program or project. Other PMOs that may exist in the organization provide coordinated, supplementary support to the enterprise PMO.

2.6 Resource Gap Analysis

Before embarking on a program or project with high levels of complexity, organizations should conduct a resource gap analysis comparing available resources with those needed for a program or project that has elements of complexity. A resource gap analysis assesses the resources, talent, software, alliances, processes, and practices readily available to successfully complete a program or project.

As part of the resource gap analysis, many high-performing organizations also conduct a skills assessment to aid in assignment of program or project managers. Using the appropriate resources and assigning people with appropriate skills, knowledge, and experience to programs and projects should facilitate the ability to navigate complexity. An example of a resource gap analysis template is shown in Table 2-1.

2.7 Senior Management, Practitioner, and Team Competency

Ensuring assignment of competent resources is critical to the successful execution of programs and projects. The assignment of competent resources includes assigning the right people to the right programs and projects. Effective management in a program or project with complexity requires enhanced program and project management

Table 2-1. Resource Gap Analysis Example

Resource Gap Analysis					
Date of resource gap analysis: Version:					
Project name:			Project ID:		
Objectives of project:					
Scope of project (if defined):					
Description of Target Project Resource Requirements	**Current Available Resources for this Project**	**Gaps Identified**	**Implications**	**Actions to Address Gaps/ Next Steps**	**Timeline**
Skills:					
Tools/equipment:					
Software:					
Alliances:					
Process:					
Practices:					
Other considerations:					

competencies which include strategic and business management, technical project management, and leadership skills (see Figure 2-1). PMI's *Pulse of the Profession™ In-Depth Report: Navigating Complexity* suggests that developing practitioners with exceptional leadership skills has a significant impact on an organization's ability to successfully deliver programs and projects, particularly those with complexity.

In general, the following fundamental skills are essential and helpful:

- **Expertise.** Defined as the expert skill and knowledge in an application area, subject matter, discipline, industry, etc., as appropriate for the activity being performed. The following items should be considered:
  - ○ Expertise may be more important than having acquired specific skills in the context of programs or projects with complexity, as it is based on prior experience.
  - ○ Expertise is acquired over a period of time.
  - ○ Decision making relies on collaboration with various experts to yield a more effective approach.
  - ○ Leveraging previous experience is helpful in managing the next program or project.
- **Adaptability.** Defined as the ability to adjust to a changing environment or situation and to adopt a flexible approach that shifts according to the situation. Adaptable team members display the following attributes:
  - ○ Willingness to devote time to learning and understanding what is unfamiliar;
  - ○ Applying and being open to new methodologies;

2

Figure 2-1. Capability Requirements for Managers of Programs or Projects with Complexity

- ○ Providing support to and receiving support from internal key staff;

- ○ Being resilient; and

- ○ Maintaining an optimistic demeanor during ambiguous, unpredictable, or changing situations.

- **Collaboration.** Defined as the skill to effectively work with others to achieve a desired outcome by incorporating a variety of perspectives to address complex situations, including diversity of thought and approach in problem solving. Collaboration may require careful consulting and coordinating as a way to engage stakeholders and ensure that goals and objectives are aligned.

- **Leadership.** Defined as the ability to guide, motivate, and direct the team, which may include essential capabilities such as negotiation, resilience, communication, problem solving, critical thinking, and interpersonal skills.

- **Strategic and Business Management.** Defined as the ability to see the high-level overview of the organization and effectively negotiate and implement decisions and/or actions that support strategic, alignment, and innovation. This ability may include working knowledge of other functions such as finance, marketing, and operations.

- **Technical Project Management.** Defined as the skills to effectively apply project management knowledge and product or industry expertise to deliver desired outcomes for programs or projects.

The right combination of attributes and competencies for program and project success needs to be determined for each environment and each initiative.

3

ENCOUNTERING COMPLEXITY

3.1 Three Categories of Complexity

Throughout history, most programs and projects have contained elements of complexity. Using fundamental program and project management approaches has proven effective in taking care of the influences of these complexities and delivering successful outcomes. In today's world, as supply chains, markets, and technology become global, program and project managers are increasingly encountering more and more complexity in programs and projects. Fundamental, rapid changes in societies and economies, including innovations in the manufacturing and delivery of products, have increased complexity dramatically in programs and projects. The anticipation of the effects of complexity and the management of actions to meet the challenges of complexity require understanding its causes and how it is experienced.

Programs and projects with complexity may fluctuate between conditions of relative stability and predictability to instability and uncertainty. Further, the organization's prior experience, talent management, and effective communications will often influence the perception of complexity and its influence on the program or project. In project management literature, there have been many views of complexity classified as: key aspects, types, dimensions, characteristics, or factors of complexity (see Appendix X2) [10, 11, 12].

For the purposes of this practice guide, the causes of complexity in programs and projects have been grouped into three broad categories: human behavior, system behavior, and ambiguity. Almost any causes of complexity in a program or project may be described under these three categories. Figure 3-1 provides an overview of the causes of complexity as associated with each category.

3.2 Human Behavior

Human behavior is the source of complexity that may arise from the interplay of conducts, demeanors, and attitudes of people. These behaviors may be the result of factors such as changing power relationships, political influence, and individuals' experiences and perspectives. These factors may hinder the clear identification of goals and objectives.

Program and project work consists primarily of the combined efforts of many individuals to accomplish established objectives. It is rare that one person's efforts are isolated from those of team members and other stakeholders. While effective interactions among stakeholders contribute to success, the diversity, influence, and number of stakeholders involved in those interactions contribute to the complexities encountered in the program or project.

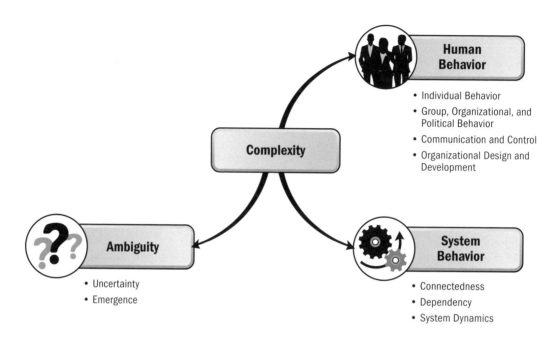

Figure 3-1. Three Categories of Complexity and Associated Causes

Human behaviors in a program and project usually give rise to complexity. Conditions similar to those in the following list may produce complexity:

- Stakeholders have set unrealistic and unachievable expectations during program and project selection and chartering.

- Key stakeholders (both internal and external) indicate significant misunderstanding of, and/or disagreement with, goals, benefits, decision processes, and outcomes.

- Clear, cohesive, visible, and active executive and organizational support does not exist.

- Unstated or concealed agendas drive decision making.

- A key team member or program or project manager is offered a gift from the client in order to have a deliverable expedited.

- Key stakeholders' representatives are being replaced during the duration of the program or project.

- Senior executives or governance boards do not give program or project managers and team leaders the requisite authority to take acceptable risks, make key decisions, or provide a process for expediting those decisions.

- The organization and its human resources have insufficient experience in the work being undertaken by the program or project.

- The program or project team has not effectively addressed interdisciplinary process integration.

- The program or project is underfunded or lacks adequate reserves.

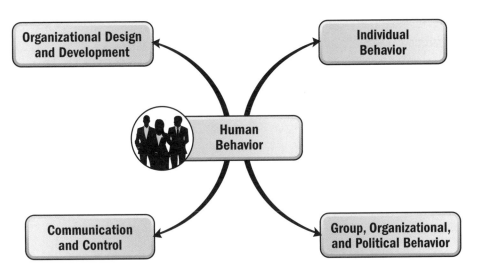

Figure 3-2. Causes of Complexity Pertaining to Human Behavior

- Critical information is knowingly withheld, postponed, or not acknowledged in a timely manner.

Such conditions of complexity may be especially challenging for the practitioner responsible for the program or project when the stakeholders are external to the organization's reporting structure. An example is a government contract project where the government officials, contractors, and the contracting organization, as well as others, have different expectations about the project. These different expectations may create openings for disagreements and unwritten or tacit agreements. These conditions result from a mixture of human behaviors, the most pertinent of which are shown in Figure 3-3 and are discussed in Sections 3.2.1 through 3.2.4.

3.2.1 Individual Behavior

When individuals act, they do so both on their own behalf and on behalf of the groups and organizations that they represent or with which they identify. The behavior of the individual becomes part of the complexity of the program or project; however, human behaviors are neither always rational nor deliberate. This section examines examples of individual behavior that contribute to complexity by inadvertently introducing elements of irrationality. Examples include:

- **Optimism bias and planning fallacy.** Optimism bias is the natural tendency of individuals to believe that they are less likely than others to experience negative outcomes. An extension of optimism bias is planning fallacy. Planning fallacy results when an individual tends to underestimate probable costs and time and overestimate probable benefits of efforts in which they or their organizations will be involved. This bias has negative implications throughout the life cycle of programs and projects. Consequently, senior management tends to underestimate costs and durations and overestimate organizational benefits from programs and projects under consideration. The resulting unachievable expectations put program and project managers at a disadvantage even before planning begins.

- **Anchoring.** Anchoring is a bias that occurs when great significance is attached to information acquired early in programs or projects when the least amount of information about the work is clearly understood. This lack of clear understanding affects such elements as estimates, requirements assumptions, and other types of information. As new information is developed through progressive elaboration, anchoring may prevent this information from being incorporated into the plan or could affect how it is captured in the plan.

- **Framing effect.** The manner in which information is presented and who presents that information affects how that information is perceived or interpreted. These actions have a direct impact on decision making. Stakeholders make many decisions throughout the life of a program or project; the outcome of these decisions affects the program or project direction. Senior management and practitioners should take steps to ensure that all alternatives are presented as objectively as possible.

- **Loss aversion (sunk cost effect).** When a great deal of emotion, energy, and resources are invested in a troubled program or project, people are reluctant to terminate it despite clear indications that recovery may be impossible. This bias affects decisions about human resource reliance, procurement efforts, and the continuation of programs and projects despite persistent failures. Accumulated data indicate that such reluctance continues despite evidence showing that a program or project will never be able to attain the business value once envisioned for it by those who chartered the program or project.

- **Resistance.** All programs and projects produce deliverables that result in change—change for the end user, change for the sponsoring organization, and change for other stakeholder organizations. There may even be changes during the conduct of the program or project in order to produce the desired end result, for example, new technology being used or new processes being tried and implemented. As noted in *Managing Change in Organizations: A Practice Guide*, it is not necessarily the change itself that is difficult for individuals to embrace but rather the transition to the change. Transitioning from one state to another involves letting go of the familiar (with its known consequences, good or bad) and accepting something new (with unknown consequences, good or bad). It involves changes in human behavior and occasional changes in corporate culture, which increase the degree of a program's or project's complexity.

- **Misrepresentation.** Misrepresentation is the act of knowingly conveying false information to achieve desired ends. This typically occurs in circumstances with significant political pressures and/or economic incentives, in which case misleading others seems to be the most desirable course of action [13]. Much of this misrepresentation may take the form of deliberate underestimation of an effort's cost and schedule, particularly in an attempt to maintain or bolster an organization's budget. Other types of misrepresentation may involve a deliberate overestimation of costs and schedules, particularly when developing bottom-up budgets (also known as "sandbagging"). Both forms put undue pressures on the organization's program, project, and functional managers by creating false expectations that may affect a host of outcomes including: organizational financial and human resources management; portfolio, program, and project management; and client and customer satisfaction. Misrepresentation on the part of the practitioner may also be due to fear of repercussions and a belief that they can turn it around on their own.

3.2.2 Group, Organizational, and Political Behavior

There are five examples of group or organizational behaviors that may contribute to complexity in programs and projects. Examples of these behaviors include:

- **Tribal mindset.** Tribal mindset involves rivalries with members of other groups. More commonly, it reveals itself as an "us vs. them" mentality between different units within or across organizations, programs, or projects, which can thwart common goals and objectives.

- **Groupthink.** Groupthink is a phenomenon in which the group's desire to achieve conformity and harmony takes precedence over rational decision making. Groupthink can lead groups to ignore essential information that runs contrary to their beliefs. It can also lead to reinforcement of tribal mindset.

- **Groupshift.** Viewed by some as a specific form of groupthink, groupshift is a phenomenon in which discussions among the group lead individuals to take more extreme positions than normal. In some instances, this results in more risk-averse approaches; however, in far more instances, this results in an increase in risk-seeking behavior.

- **Self-organization.** People have a natural tendency to self-organize. In programs and projects, people may decide to band together in ways that may or may not align with the established program or project organization. Self-organization could prove to be beneficial and/or detrimental to program and project outcomes.

- **Lack of stakeholder commitment.** It is difficult for a program or project to achieve success without the explicit commitment and support of its key stakeholders. Stakeholders serve a variety of functions in a project, such as defining requirements (e.g., clients, customers, and end users), supplying needed resources (e.g., functional or resource managers), and championing the program or project to senior management and within the organization (sponsors). The commitment of key stakeholders is often minimal or nonexistent. Reasons for lack of commitment vary widely and may include some of the examples previously cited (misrepresentation and hidden agendas) or other reasons involving organizational politics and personal agendas. In some instances, commitment on the part of some stakeholders may vary depending upon the probable success of the project. Wavering stakeholder commitment may create the uncertainty that, in turn, increases the degree of complexity in a project.

3.2.3 Communication and Control

Geographical dispersal of the program or project team, client, suppliers, and other key stakeholders creates complexities for practitioners in communication and control. While colocation is ideal, it rarely occurs in today's ever-changing business environment. Virtual teams are becoming the norm rather than the exception. Project teams and stakeholders are spread across the globe, in political entities with differing regulatory and business environments. Some examples of complexities in communication and control include the following:

- **Varying legal perspectives.** Laws have developed over the centuries and reflect a society's perspective on ethics and morality. Naturally, legal considerations vary from country to country and these differences present complexities in planning and control for program and project managers. Not only can laws be open to varying interpretations, but what's legal in some countries may not be legal in others. This opens the door for potential misinterpretation and ethical dilemmas for the delivery manager. For example, in many countries, offering money or favors to public officials in order to affect their behavior in ways favorable to oneself or one's organization is punishable by law. However, in other countries, this conduct is neither diligently prosecuted by the authorities nor conceived by society as unethical. Further, such behavior may be a prerequisite for conducting business.

- **Cultural diversity.** Cultures vary from country to country and even within individual countries. These differences may affect common understanding as well as how stakeholders communicate and interact with one and other. They may even affect whether stakeholders trust each other. There are various cultural dimensions that could increase complexity when a program or project is conducted in a cross-cultural environment; these may include the tolerance for inequality in levels of authority in organizations and institutions, the degree to which people tend to operate within a group or autonomously, the distribution of roles between men and women, or the levels of comfort with unstructured situations [14].

3.2.4 Organizational Design and Development

The organization's structure, managerial authority, process design, reporting relationships, numbers and experience of team members, education, and training of staff may each contribute to the degree of complexity of a program or project. Two examples of complexity associated with organizational design and development are misalignment and opacity.

- **Misalignment.** There are various types of fit or alignment that, if not appropriate, may lead to an increase in the degree of complexity in a program or project. Such misalignment may occur:

  - Between the program or project and the organization's strategic goals. The probability of misalignment may increase without the presence of an effective portfolio management process.

  - Between the features of governance and the types of programs and projects that an organization undertakes in pursuit of its goals.

  - Between any authorized program or project and the organization's ability to staff it, either internally or through external means with sufficient numbers of appropriately skilled resources.

  - Among stakeholders and the program or project goals and objectives.

At the outset of the program or project, misalignment may be the reality with which the practitioner is faced. However, once alignment among stakeholders is solidified, these conditions may be minimized. Regardless of whether new, influential stakeholders are brought into the program or project midstream or whether true alignment among stakeholders is never attained, these conditions could intensify again later in the life cycle. Such lack of alignment may result in conflicting priorities and direction for the program or project team.

- **Opacity.** The manner in which an organization conducts its business (i.e., makes decisions, determines strategies, and sets priorities) goes far toward determining the trust given to it by its stakeholders, both internal and external. Hidden agendas, secretive decision-making processes, and suspect promotion and reward processes may inevitably lead to a lack of trust by a program's or project's stakeholders. If these processes are not transparent, consequent mistrust of the organization by program or project team members and mistrust among team members may lead to complexities that the practitioner encounters when assembling and managing the program or project team.

3.3 System Behavior

Programs and projects may be viewed as systems existing within other systems. In a complex environment, programs and projects are interdependent through connections among their parts or components. As an example, consider the project and its sponsoring organization, which may include systems such as human activities, organizational structures, organizational processes, and rules of engagement. Complexity can occur as a result of component connections and when there are disconnects among these components.

For the purposes of this practice guide, a system is considered to be a collection of different components that together can produce results not obtainable by the components alone. A component is an identifiable element within the program or project that provides a particular function or group of related functions. As multiple changes occur in the system and between the system and its environment, adaptive behavior occurs within the components, which in turn adds to the system's dynamics.

Any system can be decomposed into a hierarchy of levels, each of which is less complex than the level above it. Significant complexity is added to a program or project as the number of components increases. In a complex system, complete decomposition may not be possible. Levels are populated by components whose properties define the level in question.

A relationship may also exist between one program and another, between one project and another, and/or between a program and a project. Program and project components may be interconnected by miscellaneous links, each having unique characteristics. As a result of these connections, changes at the component level may create unintended consequences throughout the program or project. Due to system behavior, any action by or within a program or project component may cause system changes.

Causes of complexity in programs and projects, under system behavior, are illustrated in Figure 3-3 and are discussed in Sections 3.3.1 through 3.3.3.

3.3.1 Connectedness

Connectedness denotes a relationship that exists between two or more components of a program or project. These relationships can create complexity in several ways:

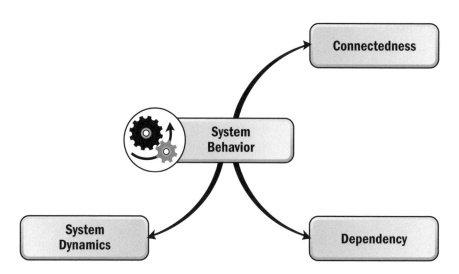

Figure 3-3. Causes of Complexity under System Behavior

Complexity increases with the number of connections. If n is the number of connected components, the number of connections can increase by $n*(n-1)/2$. When large numbers of seemingly unrelated components are connected, then complexity increases significantly. The nature of these connections may also be quite important. For example, the complexity in a program or project may be amplified with the number of stakeholders such as regulatory agencies, licensing approval authorities, quality assurance and quality control consultants, local and international investors, international financial institutions, multiple vendors, numerous specialty subcontractors, nongovernmental organizations (NGOs), or local communities. These stakeholders can have a significant impact on the structural complexity of the program or project. Examples include defense programs, large construction projects, space programs, and government restructuring programs, etc.

Complexity may also increase with the number of missing connections between program or project components. Missing connections could be missing communications or information channels, undeveloped links, or disconnects among components over time, etc. For example, when the program or project manager is not included in a crucial communication, there is a potential for increased miscommunication as well as the potential for unintended consequences.

Attempts to simplify the connections for a stakeholder group without proper analysis of the existing dependencies may also increase complexity in the program or project. For example, when multiple organizations form a consortium or a joint venture in order to deliver a program or project, the new organization hierarchies and decision processes become significantly more complex due to the inevitable new multilevel component connections. Complexity may arise due to the different organizational components such as people, PMOs, program and project teams, sponsors, financial institutions, functional departments of the partners, and various methodologies. This is particularly true for large programs or projects due to sharing of resources and competing priorities, etc. The necessary attempts to simplify and align these connections must be well planned and communicated.

3.3.2 Dependency

Dependency is a potential cause of complexity. Some programs or projects have a high degree of dependency with other programs or projects and, in some cases, it is impossible to design work packages that are fully independent of each other. Further, as this dependency grows, program or project complexity may increase significantly.

Dependency occurs when work packages are dependent on other work packages. Some work packages cannot start until one or more work packages are completed; also some work packages cannot start until other work packages start. The greater the number of dependencies among schedule activities, the more complexity is likely to be encountered within the project. Further, as complexity increases, governance and management of the program or project may become intertwined.

Critical path analysis of the program or project also becomes more challenging due to dependency. For example, in projects, the percentages of work packages that have no float or have multiple or parallel critical paths are especially sensitive to failure. With programs, similar statements can be made regarding projects that form the critical path of the program.

The following are examples of dependencies that may cause complexity.

- **Dependency between the program or project and the environment in which the program or project operates.** Changes between the program and project may impact the environment; and, in the same way, the environment may impact the program and project. For example, unexpected weather patterns may impact the launch date of a space program.

- **Dependency between the program and project.** For example, a building program at an airport may include the addition of a new concourse and parking facility; each is considered as a separate project, but each project is part of the program because the parking facility is required to accommodate the increased usage of the airport facility. An unexpected change in security requirements for the parking facility requires a modification of the project. This modification impacts the overall program completion due to the overall usage date of the facility.

- **Overlooked dependency internal and external to the program or project.** Overlooked dependency refers to the potentially hidden connections among individual components in a hierarchical system. For example, dependencies between work packages in different parts of a work-breakdown-structure (WBS) hierarchy may go unnoticed with a consequent failure to identify the full scope of the project. Depending upon the communication and control structure of the program or project (see Section 3.2.3), this may also lead to dysfunctional individual or group behavior.

3.3.3 System Dynamics

System dynamics result from the connectedness and interdependency of many components that interact so as to cause change over time. The interactions among components of the system may cause interconnected risks, draw on resources, create emerging, unforeseeable issues, and unclear and disproportional cause-and-effect relationships. An example of system dynamics is the impact of replacing a key person, such as a team lead or possibly the project manager with a person having different qualities and skills.

Organizations, stakeholders, and program or project teams rarely act in isolation. Various stakeholders (e.g., the program or project manager, team members, senior management, vendors, competitors, etc.) interact with each other during the course of a program or project. Influences, both internal and external to the program or project, will affect decisions on an ongoing basis. Instead of expecting to operate in a controlled system with deliberate, unchanging conditions and processes, those who manage programs and projects in an environment that exhibits complexity should be prepared for the unexpected. For example, the oil embargo of the 1970s radically changed the business model for the global automotive industry. Automotive manufacturers were forced to move from the design and development of large, fuel-inefficient vehicles to small, fuel-efficient models for which new infrastructures also had to be developed. Some manufacturers were quicker to adapt to the new conditions, others had to follow later after a loss of market share.

3.4 Ambiguity

Ambiguity can be described as a state of being unclear and not knowing what to expect or how to comprehend a situation. Unclear or misleading events, cause-and-effect confusion, emergent issues, or situations open to more than one interpretation in programs and projects lead to ambiguity. Ambiguity is a common aspect in programs and projects with complexity.

This practice guide addresses two ambiguity causes (see Figure 3-4) that contribute, independently or in combination with the complexity of a program or a project: emergence and uncertainty (see also Sections 3.4.1 and 3.4.2).

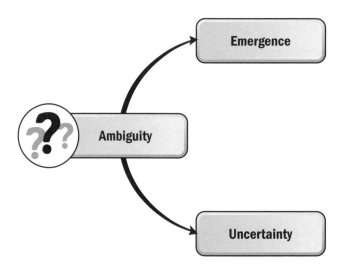

Figure 3-4. Causes of Ambiguity

3.4.1 Emergence

Emergence is the unanticipated change, spontaneous or gradual, that occurs within the context of a program or project. It may be concealed and then become visible. Emergence arises from the dynamic interrelationships among and between program or project components, for example stakeholders and/or program or project processes, to produce new, unforeseeable situations and opportunities (i.e., the whole is greater than the sum of the parts). Interdependency drives emergence and change.

An emergent behavior or characteristic can appear when a number of active stakeholders and processes interact, resulting in new behaviors or resulting in new characteristics. These interactions usually have feedback characteristics. These characteristics determine new behaviors, which may replace existing ones, thereby creating a new dynamic in the program or project.

For example, emergence is encountered when a clinical trial in a pharmaceutical project produces results that require the organization to change the positioning of a drug being developed or when a new powerful stakeholder appears in an infrastructure program or project, due to rising collective environmental concerns by the local community.

Emergence may have a positive or negative impact on innovation. Adequate risk and change management procedures should be in place to enable positive impacts and minimize negative impacts.

3.4.2 Uncertainty

Uncertainty is the state of being unsure, of not knowing an issue or situation. In programs and projects, uncertainty may be described as a lack of awareness and understanding of issues, events, path to follow, or solutions to pursue. Uncertainty may increase and amplify issues, risks, behaviors, or situations, which are internal and external to a program or project. As the number of interdependent actions increase, uncertainty may also increase. In programs and projects, the existence of unknowable unknowns and the inherent inability to address and act upon these situations may enhance uncertainty.

Managing uncertainty in programs and projects with complexity requires understanding and resolution of issues before they escalate and impact the next steps in the program or project management plan. For example, uncertainty may arise when stakeholders have different or conflicting perspectives regarding project deliverables. Stakeholder management and communication management are quite important in resolving emergent issues and risks in such situations. Adequate risk and change management procedures should be in place to enable proper actions. The emphasis should be not only on project control methods but also on risk sharing and collaboration.

Technical uncertainty may arise for program and project teams that encounter new technologies or are required to develop and apply new technologies for use during program or project execution (e.g., product innovation projects, state-of-the-art construction projects, information and communication technology projects, or research and development projects). The ability to effectively plan, schedule, control costs, and make decisions becomes more difficult under conditions of changing feedback. This may result in instability of assumptions and additional risk. In addition, new technology usually causes a training challenge and timely availability of training resources, thereby affecting the critical path. Moreover, some programs and projects use more than one methodology from multiple disciplines such as project management, design, construction, systems engineering, program and project governance, organizational change management, etc. While an individual methodology may give rise to complexity, substantial complexity often arises from the integrated usage of multiple methodologies from different disciplines for the particular program or project.

Programs and projects with lengthy durations are more likely to encounter unforeseeable events that occur with the passage of time. Examples of these changes include: managerial changes, mergers and acquisitions, bankruptcies, promulgations of new government legislation, stakeholder changes, changes in team members, requirements that are no longer valid, or requirements that have morphed over time, etc. With programs and projects having extended durations, unanticipated changes may introduce additional interdependencies, which may have positive or negative effects on the program or project. For example, a new political party in power may have a different approach to an infrastructure program causing disruption to various projects' scope, schedule, or budget, etc.

The program or project manager may need to consult experts outside of the program or project team in order to adapt to unforeseeable changes. In certain cases, some of the initially agreed-upon objectives of the program or project will be impossible to meet. Resilience, flexibility, and adaptability by all key stakeholders are required in such circumstances. Uncertainty may be a factor (cause) as well as a result (effect) of complexity. For example, changing organizational strategies may create new uncertainties for the program or project.

PMI FOUNDATIONAL STANDARDS AND USEFUL PRACTICES

4

4.1 PMI Foundational Standards

The tools, processes, techniques, and principles described in PMI's four foundational standards (*PMBOK® Guide, The Standard for Program Management, The Standard for Portfolio Management,* and *OPM3®*) form the basis for managing programs and projects. When dealing with complexity in programs and projects, these standards provide an excellent starting point for addressing the conditions of complexity brought about by issues with ambiguity, human behavior, and system behavior. Judicious and thoughtful employment of all of these tools will help the practitioner to navigate through the ever changing terrain of a complex program or project environment. According to PMI's *Pulse of the Profession™ In Depth Report: Navigating Complexity,* many organizations are using the processes and methods described in these foundational standards as part of their arsenal to achieve success on programs and projects of varying levels of complexity (see Table 4-1).

Table 4-1. Maturity and Consistent Use of PPM Techniques, Methods, and Practices among High- and Low-Performing Organizations

Project Management Techniques, Methods and Practices, and Maturity	High-Performing Organization Usage, %	Low-Performing Organization Usage, %
Risk management practices	81%	51%
Project performance measures	80%	57%
Change management practices	76%	64%
Resource management to estimate and allocate resources	82%	51%
Program management	80%	48%
Project portfolio management	76%	39%
Agile/incremental/iterative project management practices	53%	24%
Mature benefits realization process	29%	3%
Mature portfolio management practices	28%	3%
High organizational agility	28%	4%
Average percentage of active project sponsors	79%	43%
Organization has a PMO	78%	67%
Average percentage of projects meeting goals and business intent	90%	34%

PMI's extensive research on practitioners' concerns regarding complexity in programs and projects shows four key areas where significant practitioner challenges were identified: scope, communications, stakeholders, and risk (see Sections 4.1.1 through 4.1.4).

4.1.1 Scope

In a complex environment, it is frequently impossible to completely define the program or project scope in its initial stages. Scope definition forms the basis for schedule and cost baselines. Deviations from the scope baseline adversely affect schedule, cost, and other competing constraints. In the midst of the ambiguity associated with complexity, the initial program or project scope will likely undergo frequent and disruptive changes over time, presenting the practitioner with challenges in controlling both the program or project work and the relationships among stakeholders. Such ambiguity may require the use of flexible and iterative life cycles. It may be helpful to use proof-of-concept and pilot subprojects when progressively elaborating the work that needs to be accomplished or when discovering a direction needs to be reconsidered. Finally, effective use of integrated change control, rolling wave planning, requirements traceability matrices, and the WBS (for those areas of scope amenable to decomposition) will go far in aiding the practitioner around complexity's obstacles.

4.1.2 Communications

Communications continues to be cited as one of the primary reasons for program and project failure in a complex environment. Communications can affect complexity due to factors such as: multigeographical programs and projects; diverse languages, cultures, and political structures; virtual teams; and the proliferation of professional and social communication channels. Employment of appropriate communications methods, key stakeholder accessibility to needed program and project information, effective meeting management, and regular updating of work performance information may help mitigate some of the causes of complexity.

4.1.3 Stakeholders

The diversity of stakeholders' agendas may have an adverse impact on assumptions about and constraints on a program or project. Social and political stakeholder interactions may produce difficult conditions for the program or project manager and the team. Stakeholders may have strong and diverse opinions regarding processes and methods for managing a program or project. Practitioners should make every effort to avail themselves of the use of stakeholder analyses, registers, and management plans. While management of stakeholders may suffice in less complex environments, higher complexity environments require the program or project manager's full engagement of key stakeholders to enable successful business outcomes. Using the stakeholder engagement assessment matrix will further this effort.

4.1.4 Risk

Within the complexity landscape, risk management is an area that stands out as one of the most important practices. Complex conditions present the practitioner with an environment laden with an increasing level of risk—

risk associated not only with the individual causes of complexity cited in Section 3, but also by the interdependency and combinations of a program's or project's identified risks. Additionally, the existence of a greater level of unpredictable, unidentifiable, emergent risk presents a particular challenge to the practitioner. Early risk analysis and assessment followed by continuous and iterative risk management are conceivably the most important activities to be performed when managing programs and projects with complexity.

4.2 Useful Practices

In addition to the tools, processes, techniques, and principles in the foundational standards, a number of useful complementary practices have been identified to assist program and project managers in navigating complex landscapes in programs and projects. These practices include, but are not limited to those listed in Sections 4.2.1 through 4.2.11. As noted in Section 4.1.4, risk is pervasive in a complex program or project environment. While it is impossible to completely eliminate complexity, it is possible to address some of its more obvious causes and to enable the organization to be better able to navigate a complex landscape. The following useful practices are intended to do just that. Equally important, these practices are conducive to building an atmosphere and culture of collaboration, cooperation, trust, and risk sharing.

4.2.1 Optimize the Organizational Structures

Senior management is responsible for creating and nurturing conditions that will enable fast, innovative adaptations to emergent changes. These conditions include organizational structures and procedures at the enterprise, program, and project levels.

At the program and project levels, senior management should empower practitioners to organize programs and projects in a manner that is optimal for the specific purposes. At the organizational level, program and project managers should generally work within the established structures. Processes that are helpful in one program or project setting could be a hindrance in another environment. Senior management should allow program and project teams the freedom to pursue these alternatives so as to ensure program and project success and attain appropriate business value.

Program and project teams may find the need to consider alternatives that fall outside of the organizational process and procedural boundaries. In these cases, practitioners should emphasize the need for exceptions to accepted enterprise processes and procedures using established organizational processes to gain such approval. In order to provide appropriate organizational structures at the enterprise level to enhance the likelihood of program or project success, senior management should recognize the need for exceptions, accommodate them, and, when possible, expedite such requests.

4.2.2 Establish Effective Governance

For the purposes of this practice guide, governance is defined as the framework for directing and enabling an organization through its established policies, practices, and other relevant documentation. Governance is essential in providing oversight and guidance for programs and projects, especially when complexity exists. In order to establish effective governance, organizational structure needs to support processes for exception handling. Due to the nature of these programs and projects, or as organizational strategies change, the governance structure needs to adjust quickly to changes and provide clear guidance and crisp decision making in the face of urgency. In programs and projects with complexity, senior management, project boards, governance boards, steering committees, or other decision-making bodies should ensure that the governance function enables and facilitates adaptive change (see Section 4.2.8).

4.2.3 Diligently Research the Program or Project Prior to Approval

Diligently researching the program or project prior to approval helps to minimize the effects of optimism bias and planning fallacy. Techniques such as reference-class forecasting, premortems, and external audits help senior management and practitioners understand the enormity of the program or project to be undertaken. Additionally, to help normalize the process, it is good practice to involve the delivery program or project manager in the estimating process provided that political pressure is not used to influence the estimates.

- **Reference-class forecasting.** This method involves parametric and analogous estimating, which includes examining similar programs or projects that have been performed within and external to the organization. It is meant as a reality check to counter the effects of optimism bias [15].

- **Premortem review (risk preassessment).** These are detailed reviews of senior management estimates by experts to consider potential risks that could ultimately cause the failure of a program or project. Risk avoidance and mitigation efforts or enhancement estimates are added to original estimates to reset budget, scope, schedule, and business value expectations [16].

- **External audits.** These audits involve commissioning a team of objective external experts to assess the validity of senior management expectations regarding program or project costs and benefits. These experts could be internal or external to the organization. For example, this activity could be performed by the organization's audit function within the enterprise PMO.

4.2.4 Match the Manager and Key Team Members to the Program or Project

In order to match the practitioner to the program and projects, three prerequisites should exist:

- **Understand the nature of the program or project.** Prior to preassignment of the program or project manager and other key team members, the organization should have a thorough understanding of the nature and objectives of the program or project and the complexities of the environment. Using a resource gap analysis (such as the one in Section 2) and a complexity assessment (such as the one in Section 5) may enable the selection of key team members with the appropriate levels of knowledge and experience. The appointment of such team members may be more effectively accomplished when the organization has portfolio management processes and an enterprise PMO in place.

- **Develop or have access to a sufficient number of experienced practitioners.** Senior management and portfolio managers should ensure that the organization has access to a sufficient number of suitable practitioners to work on the programs and projects that will be undertaken during any given timeframe. These practitioners may be employees or contractors. Practitioners may be acquired through various other means such as joint ventures, subcontracting, or teaming arrangements. It is important for key resources to be available continuously for the duration of the program or project. Commitment from senior management to support resource availability for the program or project should be secured upfront.

- **Ensure that practitioners have leadership and business skills.** As discussed in Section 2.6, effective management of a program or project with significant levels of complexity requires the assignment of program and project managers with enhanced leadership and strategic and business management capabilities. It is the responsibility of senior management to ensure that these individuals are available to meet the enterprise's needs.

4.2.5 Listen to Experts

Senior management and practitioners need to pay attention to those who are closest to the work of the program and project. These experts have the most relevant expertise and are able to provide timely and pertinent information on how to address issues that arise. The program or project manager should collect feedback from various levels and functions in order to make informed decisions. For programs and projects that encompass multiple disciplines and technologies, it is important that practitioners seek advice from those with the most relevant expertise.

4.2.6 Manage Integration Effectively

One of the key roles of the program or project manager is that of an integrator. This role takes on added significance in a complex environment. Structural complexity presents the need for integrating a significant number of interdependent elements (e.g., requirements, activities, risks, components, stakeholders, and processes). As the level of interdependency increases, the complexity increases in addition to the need for effective management of integration.

Key areas of integration management may include planning and schedule integration, scope integration, solution integration and release management, method alignment, and program or project process integration. The increased probability of change among interconnected components introduces greater complexity and may result in an increased need for, and greater intensity of, the practitioner's integrative efforts.

Practitioners should effectively communicate the vision and benefits that the program or project is expected to achieve for the organization. The program or project schedule and budget should include adequate time and cost for planned integration activities, not only for the program or project manager, but also for all stakeholders whose efforts are required. Senior management should recognize the need for additional management reserves to address unforeseeable integration efforts associated with the emerging changes that are characteristic of a complex environment.

4.2.7 Focus on Change Management

While all programs and projects require some degree of change management, its importance increases in complex environments. As *Managing Change in Organizations: A Practice Guide* states, "executives, practitioners, and stakeholders involved with the changes resulting from a turbulent and uncertain business environment need to develop a firm understanding of the methodologies and flexibilities surrounding changes inherent in the business environment."

The uncertainties that are characteristic in complex environments increase the probability that change may occur quickly and unexpectedly. As a result of the system's dynamics, the effects of change may be pronounced. Changes in a complex environment should be analyzed with a focus on thorough impact analysis as a pivotal element of the change management process. It is important that practitioners be experienced in leading change and that change be managed using appropriate, organizationally approved processes. Additional information is provided in *Managing Change in Organizations: A Practice Guide*.

4.2.8 Encourage a Resilient Mindset

Practitioners and organizations face a great degree of uncertainty when managing programs and projects with complexity. These programs and projects may experience periods of stability and instability. In times of instability, there is a natural tendency to exert a greater degree of control over the program or project team. Keep in mind that, as varying situations arise, appropriate leadership styles need to be employed. Organizations and program or project managers should create the requisite conditions for the team to succeed, which may include, but are not limited to the following actions:

- Create and nurture conditions that will enable fast, innovative adaptations to emergent changes. These conditions include organizational structures and procedures at the enterprise, program, and project levels.
- Employ a flexible leadership style, appropriate to the situation that will permit the program or project team to be as creative and resilient as required.
- Keep the lines of communication open between senior management and the program or project team.
- Make use of the right tools for maximum efficiency.
- Judiciously reduce or modify the rules, policies, and procedures as needed within legal and regulatory boundaries.
- Think paradoxically. Find creative solutions to work with diverse personalities. Acknowledge contrarian positions and incorporate them where appropriate.
- Facilitate team-bonding events and collective understanding of the project's goals and cooperative work.
- Be aware of the anxiety and emotions that inevitably emerge in complex projects, and provide support to handle them creatively and positively.
- Employ reflective thinking (see Section 4.2.11). Program and project managers should be reflective practitioners with social and political skills in order to be able to create, maintain, and influence collaborative relationships among program or project stakeholders.

4.2.9 Pay Attention to Small Signs that May Signify Major Changes

In programs and projects with complexity, even the smallest deviation could trigger an unexpected series of events with unforeseen consequences. Senior management and practitioners should be sensitive to any indications that something may be amiss. For example, a contractor's key technical lead did not attend two consecutive weekly project technical meetings and the reasons given did not appear to be in line with known facts. This situation may indicate that the technical lead is working on projects deemed more important, which may subsequently result in less-experienced contractor resources working on the project.

It is important to develop and maintain communication networks that include all key stakeholders, and closely monitor these ever-changing human or organizational relationships for signs of change that may indicate additional threats or opportunities as they begin to emerge. Critical path analysis and project control techniques (e.g., earned value) may be early indicators of changes in program or project performance (e.g., trend analysis using cost performance index (CPI) or deterioration of float on tasks off the critical path). Small changes can have significant impact, therefore program and project managers and teams should look for unanticipated results or unintended consequences that were not identified in the change analysis from any change approved for a program or project.

4.2.10 Avoid Oversimplification

People are conditioned and educated to identify specific causes for specific effects, which sometimes results in oversimplification. With interconnected and unpredictable complexity on programs and projects, effects are seldom the result of a single cause. The temptation to oversimplify can result in the ineffective resolution of issues by addressing only some of the factors that cause them. For example, program and project dashboards are frequently devised to convey current status information for busy executives who don't have the time to sift through all of the details. However, as appropriate as these dashboards may be for their intended purpose, they may lack the nuances to convey the true status of the program or project.

4.2.11 Encourage Reflective Thinking

An individual's ability to learn from experience is necessary for developing the wisdom required to manage programs and projects in a complex environment. Two types of learning that one should practice may be referred to as learning *from* the experience and learning *in* the experience [17].

Learning *from* the experience is exemplified by the development of lessons learned. Typically these are discussed, analyzed, documented, and distributed appropriately throughout the organization at the end of program or project phases and during the closing processes. Learning *in* the experience, on the other hand, takes place more immediately as the practitioner is reflecting on recent events, contemplating whether work is progressing as expected and how it might be changed to better enhance the program or project outcomes. This type of learning is documented as it occurs and is distributed quickly for a more instantaneous impact on program and project work. The wisdom developed from both types of learning happens only over time and with exposure to performing and managing in various program and project environments.

A key component to developing this wisdom is the ability to reflect on one's experiences in a continuous and critical fashion in order to apply the appropriate knowledge and experience within a specific context. Reflective thinking, a key component of the critical thinking process, is a requirement for higher levels of professional development. Organizations should promote the development of reflective practitioners through various methods including structured workplace learning, corporate universities, and project management academies, etc. [12].

5

NAVIGATING COMPLEXITY: THE ASSESSMENT QUESTIONNAIRE

5.1 Assessing and Navigating Complexity

In order to navigate complexity, an assessment of the program or project may help practitioners, sponsors, and senior management recognize the existence of complexity and identify the possible causes. Since most programs and projects today have some elements of complexity, an early and iterative assessment of complexity is needed to enable an informed view of the program or project under consideration. As noted in Sections 4.2.3 and 4.2.4, it is important to diligently research the program or project prior to approval and match it with the manager and key team members. A thorough understanding of the nature and objectives of the program or project and the complexities of the environment is important prior to the approval and initiation of programs and projects. Therefore in addition to a complexity assessment, a resource gap analysis is also critical and should be conducted to provide the basis for informed decisions.

This section contains a complexity assessment for which a negative answer may indicate the presence of complexity and encourage the user to think about the potential causes of complexity. There are a number of assessment instruments available, some of which are mentioned in the annotated bibliography in Appendix X2. Table 5-1 is an assessment questionnaire for complexity that can also be used.

The steps that the user needs to follow after completing the assessment in order to navigate complexity are as follows and shown in Figure 5-1:

- **Step A.** Become familiar with Sections 1, 2, 3, and 4 of this practice guide.
- **Step B.** Complete the assessment questionnaire in Table 5-1.
- **Step C.** Consider "No" responses in order to determine the possible causes of complexity and reflect on possible actions to treat these causes.
- **Step D.** Review Section 6 to view sample scenarios and possible actions; then reflect on how the assessment questions may link to these scenarios.
- **Step E.** Apply critical thinking as explained in Section 7.
- **Step F.** Build action plans to navigate complexity and manage the execution of the action plans.
- **Step G.** Continually assess the outcomes from the action plans and repeat the appropriate steps as necessary.

When using the complexity assessment questionnaire in Table 5-1, keep in mind that complexity may exist at many levels and should be viewed subjectively. Therefore, it may be necessary to obtain other perspectives by asking external experts and other members of the program or project team to complete the assessment. It is

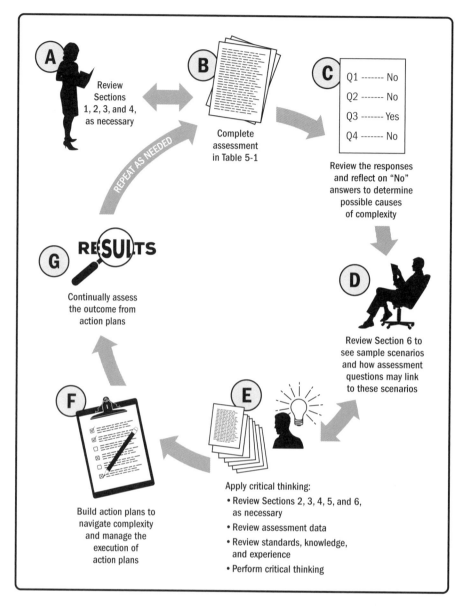

Figure 5-1. How to Use the Complexity Assessment Process

equally important to continually review and reassess the complexities of a particular situation throughout the life cycle of the program or project.

Table 5-1. Assessment Questionnaire

No	Question	Yes	No
1	Can the program or project requirements be clearly defined at this stage?		
2	Can the program or project scope and objectives be clearly developed?		
3	Are there only a few quality requirements to which the program or project needs to conform that do not contradict one another?		
4	Are the program or project assumptions and constraints likely to remain stable?		
5	Are stakeholder requirements unlikely to change frequently?		
6	Are there a limited number of dependency relationships among the components of the program or project?		
7	Does the program or project manager have the authority to apply internal or external resources to program or project activities?		
8	Are there plans to transition processes and/or products to the customer or client?		
9	Will the deliverable(s) of the program or project utilize only a few different technologies (e.g., electrical, mechanical, digital)?		
10	Will the deliverable(s) of the program or project have a manageable number of components, assemblies, and interconnected parts?		
11	Does the program or project have clearly defined boundaries with other programs or projects and initiatives that may be running in parallel?		
12	Is there consistency between what the customer communicates and what the customer actually needs?		
13	Are the program or project team members based within the same region?		
14	Is it feasible to obtain accurate program or project status reporting throughout the life of the project?		
15	Is the program or project being coordinated within a single organization?		
16	Will the program or project be conducted in a politically and environmentally stable country?		
17	Will the program or project team members primarily work face-to-face (rather than virtually) throughout the program or project?		
18	Is there open communication, collaboration, and trust among the stakeholders and the program or project team?		
19	Will the program or project have an impact on a manageable number of stakeholders from different countries, backgrounds, languages, and cultures?		
20	Does the organization have the right people, with the necessary skills and competencies, as well as the tools, techniques, or resources to support the program or project?		
21	Is the senior management team fully committed to the program or project?		

No	Question	Yes	No
22	Will the program or project be conducted over a relatively short period of time, with a manageable number of stakeholder changes?		
23	Does the program or project have the support, commitment, and priority from the organization and functional groups?		
24	Is funding for the program or project being obtained from a single source or sponsor?		
25	Have the success criteria for the program or project been defined, documented, and agreed upon by stakeholders?		
26	For a multiorganizational-sponsored program or project, are all organizations aligned regarding project management processes, tools, and techniques?		
27	Are there a manageable number of third-party program or project relationships?		
28	Has this type of program or project ever been undertaken by the organization?		
29	Are the actual rate and type or propensity for change manageable?		
30	Does the program or project have a manageable number of issues, risks, and uncertainties?		
31	Are the legal or regulatory requirements to which the program or project must comply manageable?		
32	Will suppliers be able to meet commitments to the program or project?		
33	Is there a high degree of confidence in the estimate to complete (ETC) for the program or project?		
34	Have realistic expectations been set around the program or project success criteria?		
35	Will the program or project deliver to the committed deadlines?		
36	Is the client prepared to accept and sign off on the deliverables?		
37	Are the program or project documents and files being kept current in an accessible location for the team (e.g., plan baseline, final plan, change authorizations, payments, correspondence, or contracts)?		
38	Have all contracts related to the program or project been free of any claims filed by suppliers or customers?		
39	Have all parts of the program or project been free from any financial penalties?		
40	Is an agreed framework in place for financial tracking at a work package level?		
41	Are the program or project metrics appropriate, stable, and reported regularly?		
42	Is there a high level of confidence that new information generated from progressive elaboration is captured appropriately in the program or project plan?		
43	Is there a high level of confidence that the interconnected components of the program or project will perform in a predictable manner?		

No	Question	Yes	No
44	Is it possible to terminate, suspend, or cancel a program or project activity when there is evidence that achievement of the desired outcome is not possible?		
45	Are team members or stakeholders able to accept the program or project data or information that may be contrary to their beliefs, assumptions, or perspectives?		
46	Is there an effective portfolio management process within the organization to facilitate strategic alignment and enable successful delivery of programs and projects?		
47	Does the sponsor organization or project organization conduct its business (e.g., make decisions, determine strategies, set priorities, etc.) in a manner that promotes transparency and trust among its internal and external stakeholders?		
48	Are there a manageable number of critical paths in the program or project?		

The actions to take following the completion of the assessment depend on many factors, which are unique to each program or project. These actions will be very specific to the particular circumstances and situation of the program or project, and a single question should not be considered in isolation. This assessment is intended to encourage the user to think about the possible causes of complexity (see Section 3) for the program or project. In addition, these activities will help inform the development of the action plan. When answering some of the questions in the assessment, the user will need to determine whether a particular attribute of the program or project is "manageable" based on the skills and experience of the team (or potential team) members and the selected program or project manager.

It would be useful to supplement the questionnaire with additional questions that cover factors specific to a respective industry, organization, or domain relevant to the program or project. These supplemental questions need to be considered along with the main questionnaire.

The intention is for the questionnaire to be revisited, as necessary, depending on the complexity that may emerge and change throughout the life cycle of the project or program.

Answers to this questionnaire do not provide a definitive answer as to whether or not the program or project has elements of complexity or what the causes of complexity are in the program or project. The responses however, are intended to help the user reflect on elements of complexity and possible causes of complexity and what actions may be needed. With awareness and understanding, the ability to choose appropriate actions and proactively manage the effects of complexity is enhanced.

Section 6.2 provides an example of the mapping between the assessment questions from this section and the possible causes of complexity from Section 3. This example may be used as a means to review and eliminate causes of complexity based on the circumstances and environment of the program or project being assessed.

In addition, the guidance from Section 2 (Organizational Considerations), Section 3 (Encountering Complexity), Section 4 (PMI Foundational Standards and Useful Practices), and Section 6 (Complexity Scenarios and Possible Actions) should facilitate the creation of an effective action plan for navigating complexity as noted in Section 7 (Developing an Action Plan).

COMPLEXITY SCENARIOS AND POSSIBLE ACTIONS

This section uses realistic scenarios that could be encountered by practitioners on projects and programs with complexity. As indicated in Figure 6-1, the scenarios connect the responses from the assessment in Section 5 with possible actions for consideration.

6

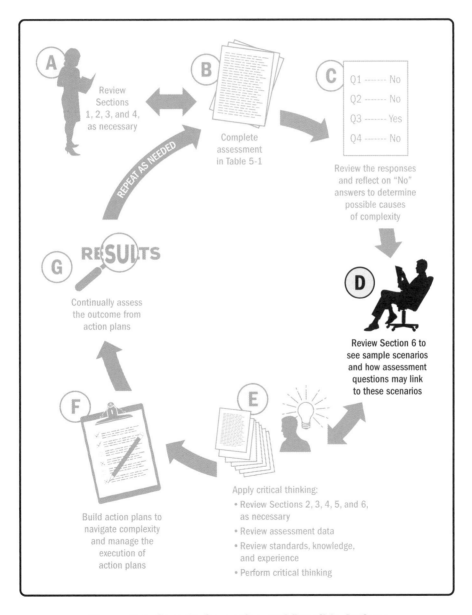

Figure 6-1. Sample Scenarios and Possible Actions

6.1 Using the Complexity Scenarios

Table 6-1 contains a number of scenarios and suggested actions. These scenarios are presented to serve as examples of how to navigate complexity in a program or project following the completion of the assessment shown in Section 5. These scenarios are not intended to be an exhaustive list. Rather, these scenarios show how examination of the assessment responses could lead to the development of an action plan for navigating complexity encountered in a given program or project. In addition, applicable assessment questions are mapped to each of the scenarios. The actions described in the scenarios may also be included in the action plan developed for the specific program or project under consideration. Before applying any of the actions, be sure to evaluate their appropriateness to the specific situation.

Table 6-2 provides an example of the mapping for Complexity Scenario 3 (from Table 6-1) and the assessment questions having negative responses with the possible causes of complexity. This kind of mapping may assist in the development of the proposed actions for consideration.

Following each of the scenarios in Table 6-1, a suggested set of steps are described for developing an action plan specific to the program or project under consideration. A further description of these actions is provided in Section 7.

Table 6-1. Complexity Scenarios

Complexity Scenario 1	The program or project requirements change frequently or cannot be clearly defined due to conflicting information received from various stakeholders.
Applicable Assessment Question	Negative responses for questions 1, 2, 3, 4, 5, 6, 8, 12, 18, 21, 22, 25, 28, 29, 30, 34, 35, 36, 37, 38, 41, 42, 43, 44, 45, 46, 47

Possible actions for considerations:

- Assign resources to verify the information received and to establish an objective basis for decision making.
- Balance and negotiate the requirements as stated by customers based on the recommendations from program or project team experts, in order to stabilize requirements.
- Scrutinize requirement changes for implications (for example, benefits, impact on other requirements) and take immediate steps to adjust the program or project as necessary.
- Put in place the appropriate program or project organizational structure to facilitate communications.
- Develop and maintain an online site to share with all key stakeholders to allow for collaboration and tracking of requirements approval.
- Be aware of small changes in the tone and context of communications among stakeholders to capture early signs of potential issues.
- Hold workshops involving stakeholder groups to understand and resolve views and opinions regarding requirements.
- Obtain the explicit commitment of stakeholders to a shared overall strategy for the program or project.

- Facilitate face-to-face meetings with a social dimension to nurture collaborative behavior and help develop trust toward a collective sensemaking of project goals, risks and uncertainty, and a shared (no-blame) understanding of consequences of scope change.
- Manage the program or project with success in mind, but always within the boundaries of ethics in the given context and personal sense of accountability and responsibility.
- Be resourceful conversationally; build collective devotion to the project through various techniques (e.g., storytelling).
- Form important personal alliances with key stakeholders.
- Develop a strong identity as the manager of projects with complexity and become established as an expert in order to gain respect and support from stakeholders.
- Arrange to meet and discuss the consequences with those accountable for original decisions and reassess risks with them against the agreed KPI (key performance indicators) for the project.
- Continually engage stakeholders on success criteria as success can change over time.
- Identify potential biases among stakeholders, understand their motives, and then develop mitigation actions.
- Conduct interim lessons learned with stakeholders to pinpoint the causes of why requirements cannot be clearly defined and manage changes to requirements.

Complexity Scenario 2	It has become apparent that the program or project is no longer going to deliver what the customer needs.
Applicable Assessment Question	Negative responses for questions 2, 3, 4, 5, 6, 9, 10, 12, 19, 20, 21, 22, 24, 25, 28, 29, 30, 33, 34, 35, 36, 40, 41, 42, 43, 44, 45, 46, 47

Possible actions for considerations:

- Create a prototype or pilot a process or service to understand the potential gaps while consulting and coordinating with subject matter experts.
- Introduce iterative development techniques when appropriate.
- Assess whether in-process change activities help or hinder alignment to the customer's needs.
- Hold value-engineering workshops.
- Consult and coordinate with team members to generate innovative solutions.
- Communicate with the customer in person whenever possible.
- Take quick action to communicate the situation and possible alternative approaches to the customer.
- Reassess scope and requirements to determine the viable outcomes that can be delivered by the program or project and seek concurrence from the customer that the change in outcomes is acceptable.
- Reexamine how customer needs relate to the strategic objectives of the organization.
- Work with the customer to identify the optimum way forward.
- Assess the viability of the program or project.
- Conduct interim lessons learned to avoid unnecessary future changes.

Complexity Scenario 3	The combination of the advanced and technical nature of the program or project has several interconnected components and/or processes that have not been encountered previously by the organization. In addition, team members do not have the necessary skills or experience.
Applicable Assessment Question	Negative responses for questions 1, 2, 4, 6, 9, 10, 20, 28, 30, 34, 35, 41, 42, 43, 44, 45, 46, 47

Possible actions for considerations:

- Compile and analyze the implications of the individual interconnected components or processes and their impact on achieving the overall objectives of the program or project.

- Consult directly with the program or project sponsor and the customer to decompose the interconnected scope elements to the extent possible. Clearly identify the artifacts and data needing to be coordinated. Reprioritize the newly decomposed scope elements.

- Request that the team take on the necessary training and development to enhance skills for alignment with the needs of the program or project.

- Encourage team members to question assumptions and constraints of the program or project in order to promote creativity and innovation.

- Conduct frequent team briefings to acknowledge and celebrate accomplishments and provide updates on current challenges.

- Ensure that succession plans are in place for key team members so that knowledge is retained.

- Encourage knowledge sharing among team members, using techniques such as shadowing and workshops.

- Engage key leaders from other functional units in team meetings and encourage collaboration by discussing how each unit can work together and achieve successful outcomes for the program or project including organizational benefits.

- Utilize technology readiness assessments to understand the maturity of the technology utilized for the program or project and the impacts on delivery reliability. Develop technology maturity to an acceptable technology readiness level (TRL) that enables reliable program and project execution.

- Include efforts for testing new technologies and the necessary system regression testing for the transition to new technologies.

- Diligently research external organizations that have successfully undertaken similar types of programs or projects in order to develop good practices.

- Investigate techniques from other industries for innovative approaches and processes.

- Undertake a resource gap analysis focused on the competency of team members and provide additional training or look for external resources.

Complexity Scenario 4	The technologies available at the beginning of the program or project will be eclipsed by new technologies required to complete the deliverables.
Applicable Assessment Question	Negative responses for questions 4, 5, 9, 10, 22, 25, 29, 30, 34, 35, 37, 41, 42, 43, 44, 45, 46, 47

Possible actions for considerations:

- Ask the technical lead to create a technology road map to replace obsolescent technologies.
- Develop alternative strategies (for example, iterative or parallel development) to deliver success in the face of unknown technology changes.
- Assess the likely costs and benefits of investing in new technologies in order to complete the deliverables.
- Include efforts that involve the testing of new technologies.
- Engage internal and/or external experts, as appropriate, to obtain a realistic understanding of any shortcomings and opportunities.
- Encourage team members to share relevant intelligence from their personal knowledge.
- Develop and implement a communications management plan to inform team members and other stakeholders of the current, updated approach.
- Focus on a change management strategy that covers not only the technical but also the consequential impact on people's behaviors.
- Provide to team members and stakeholders opportunities for training on future technologies that will be used.
- Engage the sponsor and customer in regular discussions regarding constraints and contingency options.
- Focus on iterative and parallel efforts to obtain quick lessons learned, avoid unnecessary threats, and exploit potential opportunities.
- Rigorously monitor signs of emergent risks (threats as well as opportunities).
- Conduct iterative SWOT analysis of the program or project environment and leverage potential technical opportunities.
- Benchmark other organizations that are engaged in similar programs or projects using innovative technologies.

Complexity Scenario 5	The program or project team members are dispersed globally, and have cultural, language, and time zone challenges.
Applicable Assessment Question	Negative responses for questions 13, 14, 15, 16, 17, 34, 45, 46

Possible actions for considerations:

- Include in the scope the effort needed for the development of effective team processes and behavior norms.
- Confirm that everyone understands and supports the goals and objectives of the program or project.

- Develop, implement, and verify effective virtual team management methodologies, processes, tools, and systems (for example, effective decision-making processes).
- Identify point-of-contact people in each location who have good language and translation skills in the agreed-upon common team language.
- Learn how to actively resolve conflicts.
- Establish and gain general agreement to a process for group decision making.
- Set up a virtual site for the team to communicate and share ideas.
- Nurture a collaborative team environment by encouraging a sense of community.
- Provide cultural awareness training.
- Pay attention to changes in team interactions such as reduced engagement or productivity.
- Help team members to adjust to the diversity of the group and make teamwork an integral part of the program or project.
- Assess existing cultural differences and work to facilitate synergy and leverage diversity.
- Be sensitive to varying working hours and holidays. Schedule meetings that are convenient for the team (not only to the practitioner's geographic location). Ensure all communications are clear and concise. Follow up all interactions with written communications. Use simple words that cannot be misunderstood when translated into another language. Avoid the use of slang and acronyms.
- Consider how to maximize value from "overlap" time between team members in different time zones.
- Make sure that everyone has a voice and continually encourage information sharing.
- Choose results-driven team members who can work independently.

Complexity Scenario 6	The program or project has numerous stakeholders, with disparate teams and sponsors from multiple organizations, each with their own methods and processes. There are also various third-party suppliers and the management structure and responsibilities are unclear.
Applicable Assessment Question	Negative responses for questions 3, 4, 5, 6, 13, 14, 15, 16, 17, 18, 19, 25, 26, 27, 28, 30, 32, 33, 34, 39, 40, 41, 43, 44, 45, 46

Possible actions for considerations:

- Ensure that the stakeholder management plan is the key focus throughout the program or project life cycle.
- Ensure the scope of work includes adequate stakeholder engagement activities (for example, stakeholder assessment, buy-in, management strategies, and continuous monitoring or follow-up).
- Pay attention to small communication nuances among various stakeholders that may have big impact on the future of the program or project.
- Learn and understand the strategies or objectives of stakeholders to adapt the right communication techniques.
- Create a glossary of commonly used terms to share across organizations or borders.

- Include methodology, process, and solution integration in the program or project scope.
- Apply mechanisms for delegation and federation of authority, accountability, and decision making in the project organization.
- Scrutinize small parameter changes in risk analysis, as these could have great impact.
- Actively engage in two-way communication with all stakeholders (for example, listening activities, inspiring people with the vision of the program or project).
- Perform due diligence and continually monitor external stakeholders' organizational strategy and behaviors in order to partner with them effectively.
- Consult and collaborate with stakeholders to ensure that everyone has a voice in the process.
- Partner with suppliers and key stakeholders to establish plans for communication and develop other ground rules for aligning different processes.
- Effectively integrate all of the key stakeholders' needs within the project management plan.
- Create management systems, clear expectations, and a climate to encourage the desired behaviors among disparate stakeholders.
- Provide conflict management and negotiation training to team members.
- Create incentives to encourage team work and successful outcomes for the program or project.
- Ensure risks are owned by stakeholders who are best placed to control them.

Complexity Scenarios 7	Requirements originate from a variety of sources with differing or conflicting objectives. In addition, regulatory or quality requirements may have overarching impact to the program or project.
Applicable Assessment Question	Negative responses for questions 1, 2, 3, 4, 5, 15, 18, 19, 21, 23, 25, 26, 27, 30, 32, 33, 35, 39, 40, 41, 42, 43, 44, 45, 46

Possible actions for considerations:

- Balance and negotiate the requirements in order to align and obtain agreement on objectives.
- Assess regulatory and/or quality requirements against the original program or project requirements and modify as necessary.
- As each deliverable is completed, verify with the client whether the results meet the program or project approval requirements and/or functional test criteria, and obtain approval or sign-off.
- Adopt a rigorous gate process throughout the life cycle of the program or project to obtain sign-off for key program or project milestones.
- Communicate new regulatory requirements to the stakeholders for awareness and action as necessary.
- Perform interim reviews of deliverables with key stakeholders to get buy-in before the effort has been expended to complete the deliverables.
- Document nonconformance and corrective actions on a database to share with team members and relevant stakeholders.

- Obtain agreement on the requirements and document this with stakeholders; share the overall strategy for the program or project.
- Review with procurement third-party contracts in order to handle needed flexibility.
- Work with suppliers to renegotiate the contracts to make them more flexible.
- Consult with program or project managers and team members who are experienced in handling regulatory changes within the geographies potentially affected by the project.
- Conduct program or project premortems to assess the impact of changing regulatory structures.
- Ensure that adequate legal resources are involved on the program or project team to enable responses to legal/regulatory changes in the geographies in which the project or its outcomes are involved.
- Ensure sufficient reserves to address the impact of regulatory changes.

Complexity Scenario 8	The program or project has encountered an increasing volume of change requests. People are no longer motivated to do their work. In addition, there are unresolved claims from the suppliers, customer, or contractor. Many of the key performance indicators and other metrics are pointing to the trend that the program or project is in trouble.
Applicable Assessment Question	Negative responses for questions 2, 4, 5, 6, 8, 10, 11, 12, 20, 21, 23, 25, 26, 27, 29, 30, 31, 32, 33, 34, 35, 37, 38, 39, 40, 41, 42, 43, 44, 45, 46

Possible actions for considerations:

- Urgently investigate whether the program or project is approaching a "run-away" status.
- Commission an external review of the status for the purpose of understanding the causes of the problems and the validity of the change requests.
- Consult and engage with the organization's legal department and consider seeking advice from an external specialized consultant.
- Establish a dialogue with the team to address the causes of low productivity.
- Focus on team-building activities to reinforce teamwork and team expectations.
- Meet with team members in person to discuss how change requests are impacting the work activities and take appropriate action to prioritize focus and resolve issues.
- Along with interim lessons learned, document and review environmental changes and potential new emergent elements.
- Implement stakeholder analysis as an ongoing activity, not just once at the beginning of the program or project.
- Review and update stakeholder engagement strategies for the program or project.
- Meet with the stakeholders to review the revised, baselined, and approved project objectives and requirements. Create a priority list of changes, documenting effort and planned delivery date. Maintain an open-door policy for all team members to bring forth issues, concerns, questions, or innovations.
- Engage the sponsor and senior management in the review of the health of the program or project and consider whether the objectives of the program or project are still in alignment with the organizational strategies.

- Review metrics for appropriateness and completeness.
- Consider whether team members have enough latitude and appropriate motivation to make innovative contributions.
- Consider whether team members' skills are appropriate for program or project success.
- Document and take actions to enhance which key program or project team attributes contributed to success and resolve those attributes that caused issues.
- Document and manage social-political factors that are permeated through the program or project.
- Conduct a review of claims that have surfaced during the program or project with the organization's legal and claims management departments.
- Generate a failure mode effects analysis (FMEA) that will identify potential severity, effect, and impact (to the organization) associated with all questionable claims.

6

Complexity Scenario 9	The project is unlikely to meet the agreed dates due to the numerous dependencies and relationships and lack of supplier or contractor commitment to the dates. This is compounded by the amount of change that the project is encountering.
Applicable Assessment Question	Negative responses for questions 1, 2, 3, 4, 5, 6, 8, 10, 12, 15, 16, 18, 19, 21, 22, 25, 26, 27, 28, 29, 30, 31, 32, 33, 34, 35, 36, 37, 38, 39, 40, 41, 42, 43, 44, 45, 46, 47, 48

Possible actions for considerations:
- Implement a rigorous change management process and ensure that each change is reviewed and assessed for impact and that all implications are understood before agreement.
- Verify the validity of dependencies and relationships among the tasks, activities, and projects.
- Examine the program or project network diagram and seek alternatives. Alternatives may include changed dependencies, refined work packages, or more discrete deliverables.
- Seek advice and recommendations from subject matter experts on refined work packages and alternatives.
- Communicate with work package owners and discuss and document roadblocks, constraints, risks, issues, and opportunities regarding the difficulty in completing the tasks or activities. Explore resolutions, preventive actions, and recovery options to get the overall project back on track to agreed-upon completion dates.
- Actively engage with the sponsors to determine the most effective way of communicating with them in order to achieve consensus. Communicate vigorously with all sponsors.
- Review contracts with suppliers, contractors or customers. Identify contractual or legal obligations that may support getting back on track and seek advice from the legal department for the best course of action.
- Seek out lessons learned from subject matter experts on similar projects.
- Examine contract for financial penalties.
- Notify the legal department or senior management of potential contractual issues. Apply rigorous claims management procedures.

- Communicate with other appropriate stakeholders regarding changes to deliverables and due dates.
- Engage with stakeholders to make sure they have provided input to the documented requirements, including criteria for success or completion.
- Conduct more frequent stand-up (or remote) meetings to address risks, issues, and opportunities that impact the agreed-upon dates for the project.
- Work with the suppliers to gain commitments to the necessary dates. Explore the roadblocks, constraints, risks, alternatives, and opportunities and determine the resolutions and remedies.
- Evaluate and document the severity of the impact of the supplier's lack of commitment to the program or project.
- Determine, document, and implement those actions which will help to reduce the impact of the supplier's lack of commitment to the project.

Complexity Scenario 10	The degree of complexity encountered in the program or project is impeding efforts at performance assessment and reporting.
Applicable Assessment Question	Negative responses for questions 1, 2, 3, 4, 5, 6, 7, 11, 14, 18, 21, 23, 25, 26, 27, 37, 38, 39, 40, 41, 42, 43, 44, 45, 46

Possible actions for considerations:

- Determine and document the necessary data and information needed to understand progress on the program or project. Verify that work packages, deliverables, and corresponding metrics are defined adequately to determine progress.
- Determine and document the roadblocks, constraints, risks, issues, and opportunities regarding the difficulty in providing assessments and reporting of progress on the program or project.
- Conduct more frequent mandatory stand-up (or remote) meetings with people responsible for tasks or activities due in the near term to report on, discuss, and assess project status. The meetings can be reduced in frequency once an agreed-upon assessment and reporting process is in place and functioning adequately.
- Communicate results of the daily stand-up meeting to all stakeholders.
- Conduct deliverable assessments with the team to ensure completeness and acceptability.
- Provide appropriate stakeholders with information on the difficulty in reporting and assessing progress on the program or project and seek their help in remedying the situation.
- Follow up with stakeholders on the success or failure of remedies and seek additional help as needed.
- Evaluate and document the project impact for absence of progress reporting and assessment.
- Focus on lessons learned to establish stakeholder alignment and scope acceptance earlier in the process in order to reduce risk.
- Develop, implement, and monitor an action plan for improving program or project metrics and reporting.
- Conduct program or project peer reviews to obtain insight into ways to improve reporting.
- Assess the skill level of the program or project manager and team to pinpoint weaknesses and strengths and to take appropriate action.

Complexity Scenario 11	The project is funded from various sponsors and sources each with their own objectives and agendas.
Applicable Assessment Question	Negative responses for questions 1, 2, 3, 4, 5, 6, 11, 18, 19, 20, 21, 24, 25, 26, 27, 30, 32, 33, 34, 37, 38, 39, 40, 41, 42, 45, 46

Possible actions for considerations:

- Analyze and define the project scope, negotiating the boundaries and deliverables between sponsors. Obtain and document sponsor acceptance.
- Develop and document the approach with sponsors in order to obtain agreement on the scope changes.
- Actively engage with the sponsors to determine the most effective way of communicating with them in order to achieve consensus.
- Mediate between the sponsors and work toward a mutual understanding of all points of view.
- Conduct regular sponsor meetings to discuss the program or project issues, risks, and progress. This becomes even more critical with increasing budget constraints and schedule demands.
- Be ever vigilant for changes in stakeholder attitudes and actions.
- Pay close attention to changes in relationships among the various key stakeholders and the potential effects of those changing relationships on the program or project, its deliverables, and its team members.
- Monitor shifts in power and influence among the sponsors. Work toward finding ways to balance the program or project goals among the sponsors.

Complexity Scenarios 12	The program or project manager is having difficulty applying and acquiring organizational resources for the program or project activities. In addition, the functional group's objectives are not in alignment with the goals and objectives of the program or project.
Applicable Assessment Question	Negative responses for questions 1, 2, 3, 4, 5, 7, 13, 15, 16, 17, 18, 19, 20, 21, 23, 24, 25, 26, 27, 28, 34, 37, 38, 39, 40, 41, 42, 43, 44, 45, 46

Possible actions for considerations:

- Revisit the scope and resource gap analysis to ensure that it documents the incremental work necessary to resource the program or project adequately.
- Consider alternative approaches to produce the desired outcomes.
- Investigate the availability, costs, and schedule implications of acquiring external resources.
- Ensure that the program or project objectives align with organizational strategy.
- Ask the executive sponsor to relay the importance of the program or project to the organization.
- Enhance the lines of communication to functional managers who control the needed resources.
- Establish regularly scheduled meetings with the sponsor and functional managers to ensure an adequate supply of resources for the program or project.
- Meet with the sponsors to validate the priority of the program or project in the organization's portfolio.
- Create a team-building activity and include the functional managers.

- Provide incentives to the functional managers for meeting the resource requirements.
- Evaluate alternative plans to address the resource issues.
- Set aside additional contingency reserves for acquiring external resources.

6.2 Complexity Scenario Mapping Example

Table 6-2 illustrates how to connect the most immediately identifiable causes of complexity in projects and programs discussed in Section 3 to the assessment questions in order to stimulate the development of possible actions for consideration. Scenario 3 is used for this example. The mapping results are subjective and may change over time with changes in the program or project.

Table 6-2. Complexity Scenario Mapping Example

Scenario #3	The combination of the advanced and technical nature of the program or project has several interconnected components and/or processes that have not been encountered previously by the organization. In addition, team members do not have the necessary skills or experience.									
Applicable Assessment Questions	Negative responses for questions: 1, 2, 4, 6, 9, 10, 20, 28, 30, 34, 35, 41, 42, 43, 44, 45, 46, 47									
Areas of Causes of Complexity ⟶		Human Behavior				System Behavior			Ambiguity	
Causes of Complexity ⟶ ASSESSMENT QUESTIONS	No Responses	Individual Behavior	Group, Organizational, and Political Behavior	Communication and Control	Organizational Design and Development	Connectedness	Dependency	System Dynamics	Emergence	Uncertainty
1 Can the program or project requirements be clearly defined at this stage?	✓	X	X	X	X	X	X	X	X	X
2 Can the program or project scope and objectives be clearly developed?	✓	X	X	X	X	X	X	X	X	X
3 Are there only a few quality requirements, to which the program or project needs to conform that do not contradict one another?										
4 Are the program or project assumptions and constraints likely to remain stable?	✓	X	X	X	X	X	X	X	X	X
5 Are stakeholder requirements unlikely to change frequently?										
6 Are there a limited number of dependency relationships among the components of the program or project?	✓			X	X	X	X	X	X	X
7 Does the program or project manager have the authority to apply internal or external resources to program or project activities?										

(Continued)

Table 6-2. Complexity Scenario Mapping Example (Continued)

Scenario #3	The combination of the advanced and technical nature of the program or project has several interconnected components and/or processes that have not been encountered previously by the organization. In addition, team members do not have the necessary skills or experience.									
Applicable Assessment Questions	Negative responses for questions: 1, 2, 4, 6, 9, 10, 20, 28, 30, 34, 35, 41, 42, 43, 44, 45, 46, 47									
Areas of Causes of Complexity →		Human Behavior				System Behavior			Ambiguity	
Causes of Complexity →	No Responses	Individual Behavior	Group, Organizational, and Political Behavior	Communication and Control	Organizational Design and Development	Connectedness	Dependency	System Dynamics	Emergence	Uncertainty
ASSESSMENT QUESTIONS										
8 Are there plans to transition processes and/or products to the customer or client?										
9 Will the deliverable(s) of the program or project utilize only a few different technologies (e.g., electrical, mechanical, digital)?	✓					X	X	X	X	X
10 Will the deliverable(s) of the program or project have a manageable number of components, assemblies, and interconnected parts?	✓			X	X	X	X	X	X	X
11 Does the program or project have clearly defined boundaries with other programs or projects and initiatives that may be running in parallel?										
12 Is there consistency between what the customer communicates and what the customer actually needs?										
13 Are the program or project team members based within the same region?										

(Continued)

Table 6-2. Complexity Scenario Mapping Example *(Continued)*

Scenario #3	The combination of the advanced and technical nature of the program or project has several interconnected components and/or processes that have not been encountered previously by the organization. In addition, team members do not have the necessary skills or experience.								
Applicable Assessment Questions	Negative responses for questions: 1, 2, 4, 6, 9, 10, 20, 28, 30, 34, 35, 41, 42, 43, 44, 45, 46, 47								
Areas of Causes of Complexity →		Human Behavior				System Behavior			Ambiguity
Causes of Complexity →		Individual Behavior	Group, Organizational, and Political Behavior	Communication and Control	Organizational Design and Development	Connectedness	Dependency	System Dynamics	Emergence · Uncertainty
ASSESSMENT QUESTIONS	No Responses								
14 Is it feasible to obtain accurate program or project status reporting throughout the life of the project?									
15 Is the program or project being coordinated within a single organization?									
16 Will the program or project be conducted in a politically and environmentally stable country?									
17 Will the program or project team members primarily work face-to-face (rather than virtually) throughout the program or project?									
18 Is there open communication, collaboration, and trust among the stakeholders and the program or project team?									
19 Will the program or project have an impact on a manageable number of stakeholders from different countries, backgrounds, languages, and cultures?									

(Continued)

Table 6-2. Complexity Scenario Mapping Example *(Continued)*

Scenario #3		The combination of the advanced and technical nature of the program or project has several interconnected components and/or processes that have not been encountered previously by the organization. In addition, team members do not have the necessary skills or experience.								
Applicable Assessment Questions		Negative responses for questions: 1, 2, 4, 6, 9, 10, 20, 28, 30, 34, 35, 41, 42, 43, 44, 45, 46, 47								
Areas of Causes of Complexity →			Human Behavior				System Behavior			Ambiguity	
Causes of Complexity →	No Responses	Individual Behavior	Group, Organizational, and Political Behavior	Communication and Control	Organizational Design and Development	Connectedness	Dependency	System Dynamics	Emergence	Uncertainty
ASSESSMENT QUESTIONS										
20 Does the organization have the right people, with the necessary skills and competencies, as well as the tools, techniques, or resources to support the program or project?	✓	x	x	x	x	x	x	x	x	x
21 Is the senior management team fully committed to the program or project?										
22 Will the program or project be conducted over a relatively short period of time, with a manageable number of stakeholder changes?										
23 Does the program or project have the support, commitment, and priority from the organization and functional groups?										
24 Is funding for the program or project being obtained from a single source or sponsor?										

(Continued)

Table 6-2. Complexity Scenario Mapping Example (Continued)

Scenario #3	The combination of the advanced and technical nature of the program or project has several interconnected components and/or processes that have not been encountered previously by the organization. In addition, team members do not have the necessary skills or experience.									
Applicable Assessment Questions	Negative responses for questions: 1, 2, 4, 6, 9, 10, 20, 28, 30, 34, 35, 41, 42, 43, 44, 45, 46, 47									
Areas of Causes of Complexity →		Human Behavior				System Behavior			Ambiguity	
Causes of Complexity →	No Responses	Individual Behavior	Group, Organizational, and Political Behavior	Communication and Control	Organizational Design and Development	Connectedness	Dependency	System Dynamics	Emergence	Uncertainty
ASSESSMENT QUESTIONS										
25 Have the success criteria for the program or project been defined, documented, and agreed upon by stakeholders?										
26 For a multiorganizational-sponsored program or project, are all organizations aligned regarding project management processes, tools, and techniques?										
27 Are there a manageable number of third-party program or project relationships?										
28 Has this type of program or project ever been undertaken by the organization?	✓					x	x	x	x	x
29 Are the actual rate and type or propensity for change manageable?										
30 Does the program or project have a manageable number of issues, risks, and uncertainties?										

(Continued)

6

Table 6-2. Complexity Scenario Mapping Example *(Continued)*

Scenario #3		The combination of the advanced and technical nature of the program or project has several interconnected components and/or processes that have not been encountered previously by the organization. In addition, team members do not have the necessary skills or experience.								
Applicable Assessment Questions		Negative responses for questions: 1, 2, 4, 6, 9, 10, 20, 28, 30, 34, 35, 42, 43, 44, 45, 46, 47								
Areas of Causes of Complexity →			Human Behavior				System Behavior			Ambiguity	
Causes of Complexity →	No Responses	Individual Behavior	Group, Organizational, and Political Behavior	Communication and Control	Organizational Design and Development	Connectedness	Dependency	System Dynamics	Emergence	Uncertainty
ASSESSMENT QUESTIONS										
31 Are the legal or regulatory requirements to which the program or project must comply manageable?										
32 Will suppliers be able to meet commitments to the program or project?										
33 Is there a high degree of confidence in the estimate to complete (ETC) for the program or project?										
34 Have realistic expectations been set around the business value that the program or project outcomes will produce?	✓	X	X	X	X				X	X
35 Will the program or project deliver to the committed deadlines?	✓		X		X	X	X	X	X	X
36 Is the client prepared to accept and sign off on the deliverables?										

(Continued)

Table 6-2. Complexity Scenario Mapping Example *(Continued)*

Scenario #3	The combination of the advanced and technical nature of the program or project has several interconnected components and/or processes that have not been encountered previously by the organization. In addition, team members do not have the necessary skills or experience.									
Applicable Assessment Questions	Negative responses for questions: 1, 2, 4, 6, 9, 10, 20, 28, 30, 34, 35, 41, 42, 43, 44, 45, 46, 47									
Areas of Causes of Complexity ⟶		Human Behavior				System Behavior			Ambiguity	
Causes of Complexity ⟶	No Responses	Individual Behavior	Group, Organizational, and Political Behavior	Communication and Control	Organizational Design and Development	Connectedness	Dependency	System Dynamics	Emergence	Uncertainty
ASSESSMENT QUESTIONS										
37 Are the program or project documents and files being kept current in an accessible location for the team (e.g., plan baseline, final plan, change authorizations, payments, correspondence, or contracts)?										
38 Have all contracts related to the program or project been free from any claims filed by suppliers or customers?										
39 Have all parts of the program or project been free from any financial penalties?										
40 Is an agreed framework in place for financial tracking at a work package level?				x	x					
41 Are the program or project metrics appropriate, stable, and reported regularly?	✓	x	x	x	x				x	x

(Continued)

6

Table 6-2. Complexity Scenario Mapping Example *(Continued)*

Scenario #3	The combination of the advanced and technical nature of the program or project has several interconnected components and/or processes that have not been encountered previously by the organization. In addition, team members do not have the necessary skills or experience.									
Applicable Assessment Questions	Negative responses for questions: 1, 2, 4, 6, 9, 10, 20, 28, 30, 34, 35, 41, 42, 43, 44, 45, 46, 47									
Areas of Causes of Complexity →		Human Behavior				System Behavior			Ambiguity	
Causes of Complexity →	No Responses	Individual Behavior	Group, Organizational, and Political Behavior	Communication and Control	Organizational Design and Development	Connectedness	Dependency	System Dynamics	Emergence	Uncertainty
ASSESSMENT QUESTIONS										
42 Is there a high level of confidence that new information generated from progressive elaboration is captured appropriately in the program or project plan?	✓	x	x	x	x				x	x
43 Is there a high level of confidence that the interconnected components of the program or project will perform in a predictable manner?	✓	x	x	x	x				x	x
44 Is it possible to terminate, suspend, or cancel a program or project activity when there is evidence that the achievement of the desired outcome is not possible?	✓	x	x	x	x				x	x
45 Are team members or stakeholders able to accept the program or project data or information that may be contrary to their beliefs, assumptions, or perspectives?	✓	x	x	x	x				x	x

(Continued)

Table 6-2. Complexity Scenario Mapping Example (Continued)

Scenario #3		The combination of the advanced and technical nature of the program or project has several interconnected components and/or processes that have not been encountered previously by the organization. In addition, team members do not have the necessary skills or experience.								
Applicable Assessment Questions		Negative responses for questions: 1, 2, 4, 6, 9, 10, 20, 28, 30, 34, 35, 41, 42, 43, 44, 45, 46, 47								
Areas of Causes of Complexity →			Human Behavior				System Behavior			Ambiguity
Causes of Complexity →		No Responses	Individual Behavior	Group, Organizational, and Political Behavior	Communication and Control	Organizational Design and Development	Connectedness	Dependency	System Dynamics	Emergence	Uncertainty
ASSESSMENT QUESTIONS											
46	Is there an effective portfolio management process within the organization to facilitate strategic alignment and enable successful delivery of programs and projects?	✓	X	X	X	X				X	X
47	Does the sponsor organization or project organization conduct its business (e.g., make decisions, determine strategies, set priorities, etc.) in a manner that promotes transparency and trust among its internal and external stakeholders?	✓	X	X	X	X				X	X
48	Are there a manageable number of critical paths in the program or project?										

7

DEVELOPING AN ACTION PLAN

As illustrated in Figure 7-1, this section provides the steps for the development of an action plan to navigate complexity.

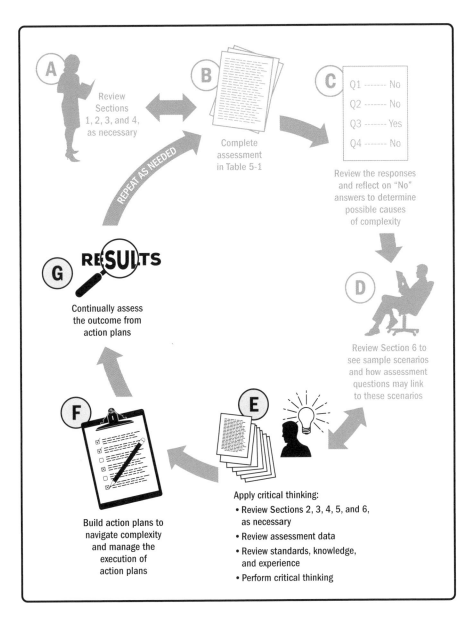

Figure 7-1. Developing an Action Plan

7.1 Apply Critical Thinking

Apply critical thinking takes the information gathered from Sections 1 through 6 and combines it with the knowledge, experience, and wisdom each person brings to the process. At this time, consider using the practice of reflective thinking discussed in Section 4.2.11. This process promotes a holistic view of the challenges facing the program or project and facilitates the following outcomes:

- Effective analysis of program and project data,
- Proactive selection of the most appropriate tools and techniques to respond to the effects of complexity,
- Thoughtful approaches to engage and influence stakeholders, and
- Development of an effective action plan to navigate complexity.

There are several steps within the "apply critical thinking" as indicated in Sections 7.1.1 through 7.1.5.

7.1.1 Review Sections 2 through 6

Review, as needed, the information provided in Section 2 (Organizational Considerations), Section 3 (Categories and Causes of Complexity), and Section 4 (Useful Practices). Then take the responses from the assessment in Section 5 and the example scenarios with their actions listed in Section 6 to create an action plan for navigating complexity in the program or project.

7.1.2 Review Assessment Data

This step uses the information gathered from the assessment done on the program or project. The "no" responses to the questions in the assessment are indicators of risks, issues, and opportunities within the project, which indicate there may be complexity associated with the program or project. List the questions receiving a "no" response. Each question with a negative response represents a situation where there appears to be some evidence of complexity. Creating a table similar to Table 6-2 as shown in the previous section may help in understanding the areas of causes for complexity and thereby aid in the discovery of potential actions for consideration. Preferably working with the program or project team, brainstorm answers to the following questions with regard to the program or project:

- Where is this situation visible?
- What is the magnitude of this situation?
- When did the situation start?
- What is the result of this situation?
- What is the magnitude of this result?
- How was this situation detected?
- Why did this situation occur?

Follow the key principles of brainstorming when performing this exercise as follows:

- Strive for a great number of responses; quality is not important at this stage.

- Do not criticize the response—simply record it (the response will be analyzed at a later step, but not at this point in the process).

- Do not discuss the responses (clarifications and discussions are conducted later in the process).

- Do not ask for explanations as to why this response is being stated.

- Record the responses exactly as given (without commenting or interpreting).

- Build on the ideas given (the more imaginative and unusual, the better).

The lists of answers to the questions for each negative response on the assessment will be used in subsequent steps to build an action plan for navigating complexity in the program or project.

7.1.3 Review Standards, Knowledge, and Experience

As needed, review standards for the disciplines of portfolio, program, and project management to gain a fresh awareness of the processes, tools, and templates employed. Search for other pertinent literature on particular issues, such as the *Project Manager Competency Development Framework* [18]. Take a personal inventory of other knowledge pertaining to portfolio, program, and project management, in addition to the knowledge associated with the industry or sector wherein the program or project resides. Finally, consider the experience of the program and project team and apply this to the information regarding complexity revealed from the assessment.

7.1.4 Perform Critical Thinking

This iterative step as shown in Figure 7-2 involves analysis, challenging assumptions, and looking for linkages among causes and effects within the system of the program or project. Take the responses gathered in the brainstorming step and organize them into logical groups. If desired, use affinity diagramming methods or other bottom-up structural approaches. The purpose of this step is to group similar items and analyze them for redundancies, synergies, and opposing forces.

Once the grouping is accomplished, brainstorm again; however, this time, generate possible actions that the team may use to navigate complexity in the program or project. Take each grouping and apply:

- Organizational considerations from Section 6,

- Standards and useful practices from Section 4,

- Scenario actions from Section 5,

- Other proposed actions generated through the brainstorming, checking the validity of each proposed action, and

- Analysis of multiple perspectives obtained from the application of proposed actions for implications and consequences of the grouping as a whole.

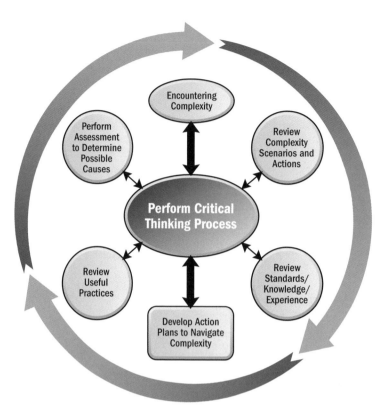

Figure 7-2. Critical Thinking Combined with this Practice Guide, Standards, and Experiences

This brainstorming session uses the perspectives gained from the participants to build links and action plans to navigate complexity. It is good practice to review the proposed actions with other members of the program or project team. Some actions for consideration may be outside of the direct control and influence of the program or project manager. As such, it may be appropriate to escalate to more senior management or sponsors.

Keep in mind that some effects of complexity cannot be reduced, minimized, or eliminated through action plans; these effects need to be managed within the context of the program or project.

7.1.5 Build Action Plans

Building action plans enables practitioners to collate the various actions developed for navigating complexity in programs or projects. Experienced practitioners know how to apply a wide variety of fundamental program and project management techniques to build a comprehensive action plan.

The following steps describe one approach for constructing an action plan.

- Review the grouping of actions prepared in the Section 7.1.4.
- Determine deliverables from this grouping.

- Determine data, resources, or artifacts needed to produce the deliverables.

- Build a work breakdown structure (WBS).

- Clearly define each action.

- Develop a responsibility assignment matrix (RAM) associated with the WBS.

- Lay out the actions into a logical network diagram, defining the relationships of the actions to one another.

- Determine the resources needed to accomplish the actions (e.g., the labor hours involved and necessary nonlabor items).

- Determine strategy for stakeholder engagement.

- Determine the critical path.

- Allocate the resources to the logical network diagram and determine the durations for each action.

- Resolve resource and schedule conflicts.

- Apply dates to the actions for a complete action plan for navigating complexity in the program or project.

7.2 Implementing and Managing the Action Plan

The causes and effects of complexity change throughout the life cycles of programs and projects. Therefore, actions and approaches will need to change accordingly. The program or project manager plays a key role in modeling a flexible leadership style, which will serve to aid in motivating the program or project team. Some factors to take into consideration when monitoring for complexity include but are not limited to:

- Duration of the program or project (e.g., technological obsolescence),

- Dynamics of the internal and external environments (e.g., key stakeholder change),

- Effects of change (e.g., many small changes that transform the environment),

- Composition of the program or project team (e.g., rotation and movement of the team members),

- Needs and desires of the stakeholders (e.g., changes associated with a competitive situation), and

- Experience and expert judgment of the reviewers (e.g., potential need to seek additional expertise).

It is recommended to take the complexity assessment on a regular basis and consider the following questions:

- Have the actions taken produced the desired outcomes? (If not, then is the approach flawed?)

- Are the supplementary questions sufficient and appropriate?

- Are previous lessons learned being applied?

- Have others on the program or project team taken the assessment?

- Is it appropriate to commission an external review of the program or project?

- Have the responses been tailored as necessary?

- Has the program or project environment become more or less complex?

The iterative assessment of ongoing programs and projects coupled with the application of critical thinking skills, the use of information in this practice guide and the foundational standards, and personal knowledge and experience should improve the likelihood of success in navigating complexity.

REFERENCES

[1] Project Management Institute. (2013). *A Guide to the Project Management Body of Knowledge (PMBOK® Guide) – Fifth Edition*. Newtown Square, PA: PMI.

[2] Project Management Institute. (2013). *Pulse of the Profession™ In-Depth Report: Navigating Complexity*. Available from http://www.pmi.org/~/media/PDF/Business-Solutions/Navigating_Complexity.ashx

[3] Project Management Institute. (2013). *The Standard for Program Management – Third Edition*. Newtown Square, PA: PMI.

[4] Project Management Institute. (2013). *The Standard for Portfolio Management – Third Edition*. Newtown Square, PA: PMI.

[5] Project Management Institute. (2013). *Organizational Project Management Maturity Model (OPM3®) – Third Edition*. Newtown Square, PA: PMI.

[6] Project Management Institute. (2012). *PMI Lexicon of Project Management Terms*. Newtown Square, PA: PMI.

[7] Project Management Institute. (2013). *Managing Change in Organizations: A Practice Guide*. Newtown Square, PA: PMI.

[8] Project Management Institute. (2013). *Pulse of the Profession™ In-Depth Report: Portfolio Management*. Retrieved from http://www.pmi.org/~/media/PDF/Research/PMI-Portfolio-Management.ashx

[9] Keuten, T. (2012). *PMI Research Report to the GEC—Key Performance Indicators and Predictive Measures Research Report March 2012*.

[10] Maylor, H., Turner, N., and Murray-Webster, R. (2013). *How Hard Can It Be? Actively Managing the Complexity of Technology Projects*, Research and Technology Management, *56*(4), pp. 45–51.

[11] Remington, K., and Pollack, J. (2008). *Tools for Complex Projects.* Surrey, United Kingdom: Ashgate.

[12] Cooke-Davies, T., Crawford, L., Patton, J. R., Stevens, C., and Williams, T. M. (Eds.) (2011). *Aspects of Complexity: Managing Projects in a Complex World.* Newtown Square, PA: Project Management Institute.

[13] Flyvbjerg, B. (2007). "How Optimism Bias and Strategic Misrepresentation Undermine Implementation." In *Concept Program* (pp. 41-55). Trondheim: The Norwegian University of Science and Technology.

[14] Hofstede, G. (2010). *Culture and Organizations: Software for the Mind*. New York: McGraw Hill.

[15] Lovallo, D., and Kahneman, D. (2003, July). "Delusions of Success: How Optimism Undermines Executives' Decisions," *Harvard Business Review, 81*(7), pp. 56–63.

[16] Klein, G. (2007, September). "Performing a Project Premortem," *Harvard Business Review, 85*(9).

[17] Cavanagh, M. (2012). *Second Order Project Management: Advances in Project Management.* Burlington, VT: Gower Publishing Company.

[18] Project Management Institute. (2007). *Project Manager Competency Framework.* Newtown Square, PA: PMI.

APPENDIX X1
CONTRIBUTORS AND REVIEWERS OF *NAVIGATING COMPLEXITY:*
A PRACTICE GUIDE

The Project Management Institute is grateful to all of these individuals for their support and acknowledges their contributions to the project management profession.

X1.1 *Navigating Complexity: A Practice Guide* Core Committee

The following individuals served as core committee members, were contributors of text or concepts:

Dave Gunner, PMP, Chair
Michael J. Stratton, Vice Chair, PhD, PMP
Carl Belack
Panos Chatzipanos, PhD, Dr Eur Ing
Carolina Gabriela Spindola, PMP, SSBB
Chrys M. Raheb, MSc, PMP
Quynh Woodward, MBA, PMP, PMI Standards Specialist

Note: Special thanks to Boeing, HP and IBM for supporting this project by providing experts to serve on this core committee.

X1.2 Subject Matter Expert (SME) Steering Group

The following individuals served as technical advisors to the core committee:

Terence J. Cooke-Davies, Chair, PhD, FCMI
Steve Markgraf
Harvey Maylor, PhD

X1.3 Subcommittee Members

The following individuals interacted with the core committee and provided input to drafts of the practice guide:

Eric Christoph, PMP, EVP
Nick Clemens, PMP
Paulo F. W. Keglevich de Buzin, MSc, PMP

Burkhard Meier, MBA, PMP
Nitin A. Patwardhan, PMP, PgMP
Vanina Mangano, PMI-RMP, PMP

X1.4 Content Reviewers

The following individuals provided reviews and recommendations on drafts of this practice guide:

Rajan Ananthanarayanan
Ranjit Biswas, MBA, PMP
Svetlana Cicmil, BSc (CivEng), PhD
Joel Crook, MSBA, PgMP
Wanda Curlee, DM, PgMP
Steven L. Fahrenkrog, PMP Retired
Theofanis C. Giotis, PMI-ACP, PMP
Patti Harter, PMP
Rahul G. Iyer
George Jucan, PMP
Kevin L. King, LCDR USN (Ret), PMP
Ginger Levin, PhD, PMP, PgMP
Rangesh Maheshwari
Mercedes Martinez Sanz, PMP
Marvin R. Nelson, MBA, CAE
Shashank Neppalli
Eric S. Norman, PMP, PgMP
Toula Roden, Master Business (Information Technology), PMP
Paul E. Shaltry, MA, PMP
Joseph A. Sopko, PMP, OPM3® Certified Professional
Kenneth David Strang, PhD, PMP
Rebecca A. Winston, JD
Sigfredo Zamorano, MSc, PMP

X1.5 Alpha Test Organizations

The following organizations participated in the alpha test and reviewed a draft of this practice guide:

Archirodon Group NV
Duke Energy
HP
IBM

Special mention is due to the following content reviewers from these alpha test organizations:

Achirodon Group NV:

Konstantinos Dikaios
Dennis Karapiperis
Hazem Sadek
Eliana Theophanous
Konstantinos Dikaios

Duke Energy:

Jennifer Baker, PMP, PgMP
Brandon Lane, MBA, PMP
Kevin Murray

HP:

Yvonne Allred, PhD, PMP
John Cole, PMP
Lou Columbo, PgMP
Norman Hunter
Theo Kraaijkamp, PMI-RMP, PMP
Mira Kukla, PMP
Trevor Marchbank
Deborah McKee
Shankar Narayanan, PMP
Craig Nash, PMI-ACP, PMP
Jes Newman
Patricia Olbrich, PMP
Aneta Segler, PMP
Clark Toohy, PMP
Kathy Walker

IBM:

Therese Andre
Marilyn Anielak
Rick Boebinger
Dan Bukoskey
Jacqui Field
Encarnacion Pitaluga Gorriz
Sophy Guo
Steve Hircock, PMP

Mingling Lee
Dietrich Lehner
Jan Mandrup
Mae R. Merriweather
Dario Perreca
Helene Quillaud
Nadine Robert-Caspar
Paula E. Robinson
Dennis Schafer
Arijit Sengupta
Brian R. Smith
Kees Vork
Thomas Walenta, PMP, PMI Fellow
Jiang Zheng

X1.6 PMI Standards Program Member Advisory Group (MAG)

The following individuals served as members of the PMI Standards Program Member Advisory Group during the development of *Navigating Complexity: A Practice Guide:*

Monique Aubry, PhD, MPM
Margareth Fabiola dos Santos Carneiro, MSc, PMP
Larry Goldsmith MBA, PMP
Cynthia Snyder, MBA, PMP
Chris Stevens, PhD
Dave Violette, MPM, PMP
John Zlockie, MBA, PMP, PMI Standards Manager

X1.7 Production Staff

Special mention is due to the following employees of PMI:

Donn Greenberg, Manager, Publications
Roberta Storer, Product Editor
Barbara Walsh, Publications Production Supervisor

APPENDIX X2
ANNOTATED BIBLIOGRAPHY—A LITERATURE REVIEW

This section provides a compilation of the literature used in the development of this practice guide.

Ackoff, R. L., and Rovin, S. (2003). *Redefining Society.* Stanford, CA, Stanford University Press. Presents alternatives to governance structures which may impact complexity in projects and programs.

American Productivity and Quality Center. (2007). *Portfolio Management: Optimizing for Success.* Houston, TX: Author. Definitive study on best practices for project portfolio management. Provides a benchmark for project portfolio management in industry illustrating the complexity facing program and project managers.

Antoniadis, D. N., Edum-Fotwe, F., and Thorpe, A. (2010). "Framework for Managing Complexity of Interconnections in Projects." IPMA Conference on *Concepts, Tools & Techniques for Managing Successful Projects,* Crete, Greece. The authors present results from a study of UK construction organizations to shed more light on the influences of complexity generated by the interconnections. The results from the study have significant implications for the way project teams are put together and managed, and enabled the introduction of a framework for managing complexity of interconnections in projects.

Baker, B. N., Fisher, D., and Murphy, D. C. (1974). *Multiple Determinants of Project Success and Failure.* (NASA, Trans.). Chestnut Hill, MA: United States Department of Commerce. Insights into success and failure factors for projects and how complexity may play a role.

Barkley, B. T. (2007). *Project Management in New Product Development.* Retrieved from http://site.ebrary.com/ lib/capella doi:10.1036/0071496726. Discussion of project management from the perspective of its use in new product development projects and the issues which contribute to complexity in projects.

Bar-Yam, Y. (2004). *Making Things Work: Solving Complex Problems in a Complex World.* Cambridge: NECSI Knowledge Press. The author, president of the New England Complex Systems Institute, explains complexity in an easy-to-read volume. He explores the basic attributes of complex systems and discusses how they affect organizational work. He suggests ways for organizations to better manage their work in today's complex world and offers case studies from the areas of: healthcare; engineering; education; the military; global control, violence, and terrorism; and improvement of developing countries.

Baumgartner, J. S. (1963). *Project Management.* Homewood, IL: Richard D. Irwin, Inc. A seminal work on project management in the 20th century. The book provides a perspective on how the project management literature has evolved in theory and practice.

Beinhocher, E. D. (2006). *The Origin of Wealth—Evolution, Complexity, and the Radical Remaking of Economics. Boston: Harvard Business School Press.* The author shows how complexity economics is turning conventional wisdom on its head in areas ranging from business strategy and organizational design to investment strategy and public policy. The author outlines an open, complex, adaptive system with interlocking networks that change organically, reflecting the interaction of technological innovation, social development, and business practice.

Berman, J. (2007). *Maximizing Project Value: Defining, Managing, and Measuring for Optimal Return.* Retrieved from http://pmi.books24x7.com/toc.asp?bookid=16115. This book lays out a framework for projects to determine value by combining the cost and schedule performance with the business value delivered by the project. He briefly touches on complexity as an attribute of a project.

Bertelsen, S. (2004). "Construction as a Complex System," *Lean Construction Journal, (1)*1. The paper argues that construction should also be understood as a complex, dynamic phenomenon. It analyzes the construction process, the production system, and the industry, as well as the social systems formed by humans involved in the project execution from a complexity perspective using a number of general characteristics of complex systems. It finds all of these characteristics present in the construction system. The paper concludes that the complexity view should thus be more in focus when discussing new project management paradigms.

Blomquist, T., and Muller, R. (2006). *Middle Managers in Program and Project Portfolio Management: Practices, Roles and Responsibilities.* Newtown Square, PA: Project Management Institute. Discussion on the results of research into the role middle managers play in project and program portfolio management.

Booz Allen Hamilton. (2012). *Improving Complex Facility Construction Projects by Using an "Owner's Paladin."* ICCPM. The author argues that for large construction projects in a complex environment the presence of a "champion" for the owner with state-of-the-art project management skills, processes, tools, and methodologies can make the difference between success and failure. He illustrates the various heightened challenges that arise due to complexity and suggests how owners can protect value by using an "owner's paladin."

Byrne, D. (1998). *Complexity Theory and the Social Sciences.* London: Routledge. The book is an introduction to the central ideas that surround the chaos/complexity theories. It discusses key concepts before using them as a way of investigating the nature of social research. By applying them to fields such as the management of urban studies, education, and health, the author allows readers to appreciate the contribution which complexity theory can make to management issues of our days.

Cavanagh, M. (2012). *Second Order Project Management: Advances in Project Management.* Burlington, VT: Gower Publishing Company. In this first book on the subject, the author explores the need for a complementary perspective for project management processes amidst the complexities of today's business environment. He suggests that, while still absolutely necessary, traditional project management practices are insufficient to navigate the rapidly changing business environment. He explores four areas of components that are vital to 2nd Order project management: having a systems perspective; experiential learning (or learning in the moment); "adhocratic" (or improvisational leadership; and reframing contracting practices.

Cavanagh, M. (2013). *Project Complexity Assessment.* Kingston: ICCPM. In his follow-up volume to *Second Order Project Management*, the author discusses methods for assessing a project's complexity. He focuses on two areas of importance—those attributes that amplify a project's complexity and those that amplify an organization's competence in addressing the uncertainty associated with managing in a complex environment. He presents a four-quadrant matrix based on those two areas suggesting which type or combinations of management approaches (first or second order project management, etc.) should be appropriately employed. He also briefly reviews other existing approaches to assessing project complexity.

Charvat, J. (2002). *Project Management Nation: Tools, Techniques, and Goals for the New and Practicing IT Project Manager.* Retrieved from www.pmi.org. Discusses types of projects, with complexity being a differentiator that impacts decisions on approach, methodology, and tools utilized.

Cicmil, S., Cooke-Davies, T., Crawford, L., and Richardson, K. (2009). *Exploring the Complexity of Projects: Implications of Complexity Theory for Project Management Practice.* Newtown Square, PA: Project Management Institute. The authors of this PMI-supported study explore the effects of complexity on project management from two perspectives: the theoretical implications of complexity science and its relevance to project management; and practical implications of discussing and debating project management and performance issues in order to develop an awareness of the knowledge and skills required to meet a practitioner's needs in managing a project's complexities.

Cleden, D. (2009). *Managing Project Uncertainty.* Burlington: Gower. The author explores the effects of uncertainty on project managers and presents an "uncertainty lifecycle." He suggests a unified theory for approaching uncertainty based on an appropriate single strategy or combination of strategies (knowledge-centric, anticipation, resilience, and learning). The book also discusses problem-solving strategies for managing project uncertainty.

Curlee, W., and Gordon, R. L. (2011). *Complexity Theory and Project Management.* Hoboken, N.J.: John Wiley & Sons, Inc. This book explores relationships between complexity theory and project virtual teams and suggests techniques, tips, and good practices for building effective teams in a complex project environment.

Dodder, R., and Dare, R. (2000). "Complex Adaptive Systems and Complexity Theory: Interrelated Knowledge Domains." *ESD.83*, Research Seminars. Boston: MIT. This paper provides a description of two highly interrelated knowledge domains: complex adaptive systems (CAS) and complexity theory. Furthermore, it provides material on identifying and measuring complexity and the relationship of complexity to engineering systems.

Enterprise Management Council (2009). *Project Portfolio Management: A View from the Management Trenches.* Hoboken, NJ: John Wiley & Sons, Inc. This work blends a story with a traditional business writing format. In the first half of the book, readers follow a new project portfolio manager who takes on a new job. The second half of the book then explains the concepts introduced in part one in a business-writing style.

Frej, W., and Ramalingam, B. (2011). "Foreign Policy and Complex Adaptive Systems: Exploring New Paradigms for Analysis and Action." SFI WORKING PAPER: 2011-06-022, Santa Fe Institute, USA. This working paper argues that a greater understanding of complex adaptive systems can help the foreign policy community by helping them rethink interconnected social, economic, political, and natural systems; the patterns and dynamics of change that play out across these systems; and the nature of human agents and their collective behaviors. Its findings in brief are the following: (a) the world is characterized by complex systems of elements that are interdependent and interconnected by multiple feedback processes, and system-wide behaviors emerge unpredictably from the accumulated interactions among the parts; (b) in complex systems, change processes are evolutionary and dynamic, are highly sensitive to initial conditions, and can shift dramatically with nonlinear tipping points; and (c) complex human systems are populated by "adaptive agents" that act in their own interests with their own view of the situation, who network with, react to, and influence other actors and the wider system. Enhancing the adaptive capabilities and robustness of these networks is central to strengthening resilience, robustness, and innovation. And for networks that are less desirable, the opposite is true.

Frame, J. D. (1994). *The New Project Management: Tools for an Age of Rapid Change, Corporate Reengineering, and Other Business Realities.* San Francisco, CA: Jossey-Bass, Inc. Explores the topic of managing complexity beginning with the concepts of chaos through to the use of methods and procedures on projects.

GAPPS. (n.d.). *Project Complexity. Retrieved September 20, 2013, from Global Alliance for Project Performance Standards:* http://www.globalpmstandards.org/main/page_complexity.html The Global Alliance for Project Performance Standards is an organization that brings together knowledge from industry, academia, and professional organizations for distribution to the greater project and program management community. The webpage cited shows the Crawford-Ishikura Factor Table for Evaluating Roles (CIFTER), which identifies seven factors that affect the management complexity of a project to permit a complexity assessment.

Giudice, D. L. (2013). "Agile Metrics That Matter." Cambridge: Forrester Research. In this article from Forrester Research, the author discusses various metrics that will be helpful to application development and delivery professionals using Agile life cycles. It is specifically cited for its discussion on uncertainty and its description of the Cynefin complexity assessment methodology.

Gharajedaghi, J. (2006). *Systems Thinking: Managing Chaos and Complexity.* New York: Elsevier. The book features the synthesis of holistic thinking (iteration of structure, function, and process), operational thinking (understanding chaos and complexity), sociocultural systems (movement towards a predefined order and the self-organizing aspect of sociocultural systems), and interactive reengineering (redesigning the future and inventing ways to bring it about).

Gladwell, M. (2002). *The Tipping Point.* New York: Back Bay. In this book that's been described by some as "pop sociology," its author describes how something small can start a trend that results in big outcomes. While not directly related to (or even discussing) project or program management, it illustrates one of the characteristics of complex systems—phase shifts—that can be seen throughout the natural world's complexity.

Glouberman, S., and Zimmerman, B., (2002). "Complicated and Complex Systems: What Would Successful Reform of Medicare Look Like?" Discussion Paper 8. ISBN 0-662-32778-0. Commission on the Future of Health Care in Canada. This paper begins by distinguishing simple, complicated, and complex problems and argues that all health care systems are complex; also in addition, all programs and projects aiming at changing a health care system are complex. Presentations of complex adaptive systems are made in order to illustrate complexity characteristics, their effects on project objectives, and suggestions to mitigate these.

Hass, K. (2009). *Managing Complex Projects: A New Model.* Vienna: Management Concepts. This book's author first discusses current thinking around complexity in the business world, and presents a model to help understand a project's complexity profile with respect to eleven project attributes (team size, time/cost, clarity of the problem, etc.) to enable readers to triage projects (highly complex, moderately complex, independent). The author also explores competency requirements for those who manage complex projects, various life cycles which lend themselves best to project complexity, and approaches for projects with various sources of complexity (e.g., long duration, geographically dispersed projects teams, etc.).

Helmsman Institute. (2012). "Why Project Complexity Matters." The paper describes the Helmsman Project Complexity Measure, a tool proposed by the Helmsman Institute to investigate and understand complexity in projects. Its intention is to help organizations have a more sophisticated understanding of the type and level of project complexity that their systems are routinely designed to handle; and accordingly to improve their ability to identify projects that require special treatment.

Helmsman Institute. (n.d.). *Guide to Complexity.* Retrieved September 20, 2013, from ICCPM: http://www.iccpm. com/sites/default/files/kcfinder/files/Guide_to_the_Complexity_Scale_v_1.2.pdf This webpage on the ICCPM website shows the Helmsman Complexity Scale, developed by the Helmsman Institute and based on a 5-year study of the Australian Department of Defence project portfolio. Its underpinnings include the use of exacting scientific analysis.

Hobday, M. (2000). "The Project-Based Organisation: An Ideal Form for Managing Complex Products and Systems?" Research Policy 29, pp. 871–893, Elsevier Science B.V. The authors argue that for delivering high value, complex industrial systems a project-based organization is required. They go into detail analyzing functional, matrix, and projectized organizations and how complexity affects these organizations and their effectiveness to deliver.

Hofstede, G. (2010). *Culture and Organizations: Software for the Mind.* New York: McGraw Hill. This landmark book examines how to better understand the effects of culture and cultural norms on the way organizations operate. It discusses: moral and ethical values upon which societies are built; and how societies regard inequality, individual assertiveness, and tolerance in ambiguous situations. This is must reading for any practitioner who manages cross-cultural endeavors.

Houchin, K. (2003). *Applying Complexity Theory to the Strategic Development of an Organization.* (PhD diss, University of Glasgow). This thesis examines complexity in organizations and within the development of their strategic initiatives. It contains a review of complexity theory and social systems, complexity attributes, types, and characteristics and argues for a complementary approach to business strategy due to complexity.

Information Technology Governance Institute. (2006). *Enterprise Value: Governance of IT Investments. The Business Case.* Retrieved from www.ITGI.org

International Council on Systems Engineering. (2010). *Guide to the Systems Engineering Body of Knowledge.* Retrieved from http://g2sebok.incose.org/app/mss/menu/index.cfm

International Finance Corporation. (2009). *Projects and People: A Handbook for Addressing Project-Induced In-Migration.* World Bank Group. The handbook describes the main business-related impacts of project-induced in-migration, and discusses the trade-offs between proactive and reactive management of its associated impacts. Dealing with in-migration of humans is one of the most complex factors in today's large international programs and projects. The handbook contains a comprehensive description of potential management approaches, including approaches to reducing in-migration, managing its footprint, enhancing its positive impacts, and preventing and mitigating its negative impacts. Interventions supporting each of these approaches are described.

Santa Fe Institute. *Introduction to Complexity:* Video, Santa Fe Institute, USA [www.santafe.edu]. A course offered free of charge by the Santa Fe Institute. The course introduces complexity as well as the tools and techniques used by scientists to understand complex systems. The topics include dynamics, chaos, fractals, information theory, self-organization, agent-based modeling, and networks. The course concludes by showing how these topics fit together to help explain the way by which complexity arises and evolves in nature, society, and technology.

Kahneman, D. (2011). *Thinking, Fast and Slow*. New York: Farrar, Straus and Giroux. The author, a psychologist and Nobel laureate in economics, discusses his theory about how the human mind works. He suggests that there are two systems or levels at which our minds work: level 1 for making quick decisions and level 2 for more complicated efforts. Expanding from his original work with coauthor Amos Tversky, their book, *Prospect Theory,* explores the limits of human rationality. This book is a must for any project or program manager and all who want to gain insight on how evolution has shaped the way we make decisions.

Kerzner, H., and Belack, C. (2010). *Managing Complex Projects*. New York: John Wiley & Sons. In this book, the authors explore project complexity from the perspective of the Knowledge Areas in the *PMBOK® Guide.* They focus on supplementing hard skills with soft skills, particularly in the area of stakeholder management (the book was presciently written prior to the inclusion of this topic as a separate Knowledge Area). They also explore ways in which major organizations have used innovative strategies to approach project complexity.

Killen, C. P., Krumbeck, B., and Kjaer, C. (2010). *Visualizing Project Interdependencies for Enhanced Project Portfolio Decision Making.* Retrieved from http://leishman.conference-services.net/resources/266/2110/pdf/ AIPM2010_0011.pdf The research reported in this paper introduces a new tool and provides insights into the factors affecting an organization's ability to understand project interconnectedness. Visual project mapping (VPM), the creation of graphical displays of projects and their interdependencies as a network of nodes and arrows, is shown to provide benefits by supporting communication and strategic portfolio decision making.

Klakegg, O. J., Williams, T. M., Walker, D., Andersen, B., and Magnussen, O. M. (2010). *Early Warning Signs in Complex Projects.* Newtown Square, PA: Project Management Institute. The authors investigated the presence of early warning signs in projects with complexity. They also researched project manager's actions on early warning signs identified during project assessments. The authors cite several barriers to detecting these signs such as optimism bias, no clear strategies, preassumptions in the assessment process, etc. The book provides advice on what the project manager needs to change to improve warning sign identification when dealing with complexity.

Kleinberg, D. E. (2010). *Networks, Crowds, and Markets*. New York: Cambridge University Press. This text's author explores "connectedness" by examining approaches from several disciplines (mathematics, sociology, economics, computer science) to better understand social networks and their impact on human behavior. While not specifically addressing projects and programs, this subject is of importance to project and programs managers grappling to understand both the positive and negative implications of communication networks on the efforts that they manage.

Lane, D., and Maxfield, R., (1995). *Foresight, Complexity, and Strategy.* SFI Working Paper: 1995-12-106, Santa Fe Institute, USA. The authors of this paper argue that strategy in the face of a complex environment should consist of an ongoing set of practices that interpret and construct the relationships that comprise the context the organization operates within.

Lenfle, S., and Lock, C., (2010). Lost Roots: How Project Management Came to Emphasize Control Over Flexibility and Novelty. *California Management Review, (53)*1. This article describes the historical events at the origin of project management and how it has developed in the last 60 years. It illustrates how complexity affects projects and argues that the discipline should be broadened in order to create greater value for organizations whose portfolios include novel and uncertain projects.

McCarthy, I. P. (2004). "Manufacturing Strategy: Understanding the Fitness Landscape," *International Journal of Operations and Production Management, (24)*2, Emerald Group Publishing Limited. This theoretical paper presents, extends, and integrates a number of systems and evolutionary concepts, concentrating on fitness landscape theory as an approach for visually mapping the strategic options a production firm could pursue. In accordance with fitness landscape theory, a complex systems perspective is adopted to create models to better understand and visualize how to search and select various combinations of capabilities.

Miller, J. H., and Page, S. E. (2007). *Complex Adaptive Systems: An Introduction to Computational Models of Social Life* (Princeton Studies in Complexity). This book provides a clear, comprehensive, and accessible account of complex adaptive social systems. It focuses on the key tools and ideas that have emerged in the field since the mid-1990s, as well as the techniques needed to investigate such systems. It provides a detailed introduction to concepts such as emergence, self-organized criticality, automata, networks, diversity, adaptation, and feedback. It also demonstrates how complex adaptive systems can be explored using methods ranging from mathematics to computational models of adaptive agents.

Milosevic, D., Martinelli, R., and Waddell, J. M. (2007). *Program Management for Improved Business Results.* Hoboken, NJ: John Wiley & Sons. This book provides a pragmatic perspective of implementing program management practices in an organization. The authors' approach has a focus on business and systems—keys to effective organizational program management. It is included in this bibliography primarily for its program complexity assessment in chapter 10.

Mitchell, M. (2009). *Complexity: A Guided Tour.* Oxford: Oxford University Press. The author, an external staff member of the Santa Fe Institute, follows in its tradition by presenting a cross-disciplinary approach to complexity theory. This easy-to-follow book shows readers how complexity theory has developed across many varied disciplines (evolution, fractal geometry, computer science, genetics, and information processing, etc.). It is a must read for those interested in understanding complexity science and its potential for helping to address unresolved scientific problems in the future.

Morgan, M., Levitt, R. E., and Malek, W. (2007). *Executing Your Strategy: How to Break It Down & Get It Done.* Boston, MA: Harvard Business School Publishing. The authors describe the relationship of strategy to projects. They illustrate the interdependent nature of many elements of project and portfolio management, including the complexity faced.

Morris, P. W. G., and Jamieson, A. (2004). *Translating Corporate Strategy and Project Strategy: Realizing Corporate Strategy Through Project Management.* Retrieved from www.PMI.org. The authors look at how to adapt to complexity through structures in the organization and governance of projects.

Morris, P. (Ed.) (2011). *The Oxford Handbook of Project Management.* Oxford: Oxford University Press. The handbook presents and discusses leading ideas for the management of projects. This book suggests that the project management discipline could be entering an emerging "third wave" of analysis and interpretation being aware of complexity, following the early technical and operational beginnings, and the subsequent shift to a focus on projects and their management.

Morris, P. W. G., and Pinto, J. K. (2004). *The Wiley Guide to Managing Projects.* John Wiley & Sons, Inc., Hoboken, NJ. Extensive anthology of writers and topics on project management. Complexity is a topic in the writing both from a leadership perspective and from the perspective of projects from concept through implementation.

MPCS. *Complexity Assessment.* Retrieved from http://www.mccormickpcs.com/images/Business_Complexity_Assessment_Model.xls.pdf This MPCS, Inc. website, a project management consulting organization in Pittsburgh, PA, maintains various articles of interest for project and business management. The specific webpage cited shows its version of a project complexity assessment.

Obolensky, N. (2009). *Complex Adaptive Leadership.* Surrey, UK: Gower Publishing. In volume, the author reassesses the practice of leadership in a complex business environment. While organizational structures have changed over the last century, there has not been a commensurate change in the leadership of those structures. The author discusses the need for leadership to be practiced not just at the top of the organization but throughout all of its levels. He discusses what can be done at the individual as well as the organizational level to develop the types of leadership needed to navigate today's fast-changing technology and economic environments.

Pollack, K. R. (2007). *Tools for Complex Projects.* Hampshire: Gower Publishing. In this important book, the authors discuss the effects of complexity on the practical management of projects and programs. They define four particular areas of complexity (structural, technical, directional, and temporal), how each manifests in the fitness landscape, and their practical effects on managing projects. The authors also explore innovative methods that are currently being used to address issues posed by a complex project environment.

Porter, M. E. (1980). *Competitive Strategy: Techniques for Analyzing Industies and Competitors.* New York: Free Press. A foundational work for understanding the world in which projects operate from a strategic perspective utilizing key analysis techniques. It establishes a sound base from which to navigate through complexity.

Porter, M. E. (1985). *Competitive Advantage: Creating and Sustaining Superior Performance.* New York: The Free Press. A foundational work built upon the author's previous work, but exploring the methods by which business can gain a competitive advantage. This becomes key to understanding projects with complexity.

Ramalingam, B., and Jones, H. (2008). *Exploring the Science of Complexity: Ideas and Implications for Development and Humanitarian Efforts.* London: Overseas Development Institute. The paper details ten concepts of complexity science, using real world examples. It then examines the implications of each concept for those working in the aid world. The ten concepts are as follows: Interconnected and interdependent elements and dimensions; Feedback processes promote and inhibit change within systems; System characteristics and behaviors emerge from simple rules of interaction; Nonlinearity; Sensitivity to initial conditions; Phase space—the "space of the possible"; Attractors, chaos, and the "edge of chaos"; Adaptive agents; Self-organization; Coevolution.

Remington, R. (2011). *Leading Complex Projects. Aldershot:* Gower Publishing. The book argues the importance to project success of key roles such as project board member, executive sponsor, project manager, client representative or team leader, increases exponentially with the scale and complexity of the project. It also combines the results of in-depth interviews with seventy successful leaders, a thorough review of existing sources and cogent analysis of both, to plot a successful course for the leader of programs/projects in a complex environment.

Remington, K., and Pollack, J. (2008). *Tools for Complex Projects.* Surrey, UK: Ashgate. The book draws on recent research in the areas of project management, complexity theory, and systems thinking to provide a reference for understanding and tackling the increasing complexity of programs and projects. The first part, elaborates on the very nature of navigating complexity in programs and projects resulting from environmental, contemporary business, and organizational circumstances. The main part of the book provides a series of fourteen project tools. Some of these tools may be used throughout the whole project life cycle. The authors have blended elements from complexity theory to illustrate why programs and projects in a complex environment are particularly challenging to manage. They build a model of four factors of program/project complexity (structural, technical, directional, temporal) by drawing upon the work of many other writers.

Remington, K., Zolin, R., and Turner, R. (2009). "A Model of Project Complexity: Distinguishing Dimensions of Complexity from Severity," in *Proceedings of the 9th International Research Network of Project Management Conference,* October 11–13, 2009, Berlin. Thematic analysis of data from 25 in-depth interviews of project managers involved with complex projects, together with an exploration of the literature reveals a wide range of factors that may contribute to project complexity. The authors argue that the factors contributing to project complexity may be defined in terms of dimensions, or source characteristics, which are in turn subject to a range of severity factors. In addition to investigating definitions and models of complexity from the literature and in the field, this study also investigates the issues of "measuring" or assessing complexity.

Saaty, T. L. (1990). *Decision Making for Leaders: The Analytic Hierarchy Process for Decisions in a Complex World.* Pittsburgh, PA: RWS Publications. The author postulates methods for dealing with complexity by utilizing better decision-making techniques.

Shenhar, A., and Dvir, D. (2007). *Reinventing Project Management: The Diamond Approach to Successful Growth and Innovation.* Boston, MA: Harvard Business School Press. This book examines projects from multiple perspectives drawn from extensive studies of projects. The authors breakdown projects by characteristics of which complexity plays a role.

Snowden D. J., and Boone M. E. (November 2007). "A Leader's Framework for Decision Making," *Harvard Business Review,* (85)11, 68–76. Wise executives tailor their approach to fit the complexity of the circumstances they face. The authors suggest that the time has come to broaden the traditional approach to leadership and decision making and form a new perspective based on complexity science. The basics of complexity are described briefly. The authors have developed, and briefly explain in the article, the "Cynefin" framework which, they claim, allows executives to see things from new viewpoints, assimilate complex concepts, and address real-world problems and opportunities.

Stacey, R. D., Griffin, D., and Shaw, P. (2000). *Complexity and Management: Fad or Radical Challenge to Systems Thinking?* London: Routledge. This book explains complex dynamic systems and covers issues such as uncertainty, ambiguity, predictability, creativity, and component interrelationships as it considers how complexity and its central principles of emergence and self-organization are being used to understand organizations.

Stuckenbruck, L. C. (1981). *The Implementation of Project Management: The Professional's Handbook.* New York: Addison-Wesley Publishing Company. In this work, the author describes how the effect of complexity in projects led to many changes in the field of project management, including how to organize for projects.

Sutcliffe, K., and Weick, K. (2007). *Managing the Unexpected: Resiliant Performance in an Age of Uncertainty.* San Francisco: Jossey-Bass. One of the attributes of a complex system is that it produces unpredictable outcomes. In this volume, the authors explore organizational risks raised by working amidst uncertainty and look at what might be done to minimize their effects. They examine the ways in which "high reliability organizations" (firefighting operations, emergency rooms, etc.) operate. Based on their observations they develop a set of five principles that help organizations develop a state of mindfulness to help discover and correct small errors that might otherwise bloom into major crises.

Taleb, N. N. (2007). *The Black Swan.* New York: Random House. This book was said to have forewarned about the economic collapse of 2008. In it, its author discusses the difficulty of making accurate predictions in a world which itself is a complex system of systems, and how complexity produces huge, unpredictable (except in hindsight) events. He shows how in all walks of life we humans fool ourselves into thinking that we understand more than we really do. A black swan is an event, positive or negative, that is deemed improbable yet causes massive consequences.

Taleb, N. N. (2012). *Antifragile: Things that Gain from Disorder.* New York: Random House. A follow-up to *The Black Swan,* in this book the author delves further into the realm of complexity and its resulting uncertainty in our daily lives. In his prologue, the author says that we need to harness randomness, uncertainty, and chaos—not hide from them—we can't avoid the unavoidable. He proposes new approaches to understanding prediction and risk management by embracing uncertainty and using it to our advantage.

Thorp, J. (1998). *The Information Paradox: Realizing the Business Benefits of Information Technology.* New York: McGraw-Hill Ryerson. This groundbreaking work describes the complexity of the field of project portfolio management.

Turner, J. R. (Ed.) (2008). *Gower Handbook of Project Management.* 4th Ed. Abingdon, Oxon, UK: Ashgate Publishing, Limited. This book is intended as an encyclopedia for project management practitioners. Complexity in programs and projects is presented in various sections of the book for example: project organization, project management processes and procedures, managing the project environment and implementing strategy through portfolio and program management.

Van Herk, S., Rijke, J., Zevenbergen, C., Ashley, R., and Besseling, B. (2013). *Adaptive Multi-Level Governance through Social Learning: River Basin Management in the Netherlands.* This paper presents a case study of a new adaptive, multi-level governance approach for river basin management designed to stimulate social learning and to be adjusted based on lessons learned and changing political and economic context. It argues that because program management environment is complex, programs should be organized as complex adaptive systems and suggests tools and techniques for their management.

Varanini, F., and Ginevri, W. (2012). *Projects and Complexity.* Boca Raton, FL: CRC Press. The authors evaluate complexity and projects from a number of viewpoints including ethics, leadership, models, and communications.

Vestergaard A., (September 2005). *Non-Determinist Vocabularies of Coping with Complex Conditions for Managing Projects Development and Change in Organizations.* Printed in Denmark, ISBN-13:9788791496772. A book about organizational development change and project management in particular. It covers implementing non-determinism in an organization, project management of projects in a complex environment, as well as the complexity of building trust and partnering.

Wheatley, M. (1992). *Leadership and the New Science.* San Francisco: Berrett-Koehler. This book is a pioneering effort in the cross-fertilization of theories around chaos and complexity sciences, developed in the "hard sciences" (quantum mechanics, molecular biology, etc.), to their application to the social sciences. The author, an organizational specialist, addresses issues involving reconciling individual autonomy with organizational order, the limits of control, and creating participative and adaptive organizations.

Williams, T. M., Samset, K., and Sunnevag, K. J., eds. (2009). *Making Essential Choices with Scant Information: Front-End Decision Making in Major Projects.* Houndmills, Basingstoke, Hampshire: Palgrave Macmillan. The book discusses complexity and the role of decision making, especially when faced with major projects. It examines the relationship of decisions to major projects and the business model, stakeholders' needs, and the processes and structures needed for these projects.

APPENDIX X3 MAPPING TEMPLATE FOR NAVIGATING COMPLEXITY

The mapping template in Table X3-1 may be used to conduct a mapping exercise. The mapping relationships may be very subjective based on the perspective of the user, particular environment, and circumstances unique to each program or project. As complexity can change abruptly, the causes of complexity should be reviewed frequently to determine applicability. However, this mapping exercise may provide insights which can be translated into appropriate actions for navigating complexity.

Table X3-1. Mapping Template for Navigating Complexity

Scenario Description:

Applicable Assessment Questions	Negative responses for questions:								
Areas of Causes of Complexity ⟶		Human Behavior				System Behavior			Ambiguity	
Causes of Complexity ⟶	No Responses	Individual Behavior	Group, Organizational, and Political Behavior	Communication and Control	Organizational Design and Development	Connectedness	Dependency	System Dynamics	Emergence	Uncertainty
ASSESSMENT QUESTIONS										
1 Can the program or project requirements be clearly defined at this stage?										
2 Can the program or project scope and objectives be clearly developed?										
3 Are there only a few quality requirements, to which the program or project needs to conform that do not contradict one another?										
4 Are the program or project assumptions and constraints likely to remain stable?										
5 Are stakeholder requirements unlikely to change frequently?										
6 Are there a limited number of dependency relationships among the components of the program or project?										
7 Does the program or project manager have the authority to apply internal or external resources to program or project activities?										

(Continued)

Table X3-1. Mapping Template for Navigating Complexity *(Continued)*

Scenario Description:

Negative responses for questions:

		Human Behavior				System Behavior			Ambiguity	
ASSESSMENT QUESTIONS	No Responses	Individual Behavior	Group, Organizational, and Political Behavior	Communication and Control	Organizational Design and Development	Connectedness	Dependency	System Dynamics	Emergence	Uncertainty
8 Are there plans to transition processes and/or products to the customer or client?										
9 Will the deliverable(s) of the program or project utilize only a few different technologies (e.g., electrical, mechanical, digital)?										
10 Will the deliverable(s) of the program or project have a manageable number of components, assemblies, and interconnected parts?										
11 Does the program or project have clearly defined boundaries with other programs or projects and initiatives that may be running in parallel?										
12 Is there consistency between what the customer communicates and what the customer actually needs?										
13 Are the program or project team members based within the same region?										

Applicable Assessment Questions

Areas of Causes of Complexity →

Causes of Complexity →

(Continued)

Table X3-1. Mapping Template for Navigating Complexity *(Continued)*

Scenario Description:

			Applicable Assessment Questions								
			Negative responses for questions:								
Areas of Causes of Complexity ——⟶				Human Behavior				System Behavior			Ambiguity
Causes of Complexity ——⟶							Connectedness	Dependency	System Dynamics	Emergence	Uncertainty
ASSESSMENT QUESTIONS		No Responses	Individual Behavior	Group, Organizational, and Political Behavior	Communication and Control	Organizational Design and Development	Connectedness	Dependency	System Dynamics	Emergence	Uncertainty
14	Is it feasible to obtain accurate program or project status reporting throughout the life of the project?										
15	Is the program or project being coordinated within a single organization?										
16	Will the program or project be conducted in a politically and environmentally stable country?										
17	Will the program or project team members primarily work face-to-face (rather than virtually) throughout the program or project?										
18	Is there open communication, collaboration, and trust among the stakeholders and the program or project team?										
19	Will the program or project have an impact on a manageable number of stakeholders from different countries, backgrounds, languages, and cultures?										

(Continued)

Table X3-1. Mapping Template for Navigating Complexity *(Continued)*

Scenario Description:

Applicable Assessment Questions

Negative responses for questions:

			Human Behavior				System Behavior			Ambiguity	
Areas of Causes of Complexity ——>											
Causes of Complexity ———>	No Responses	Individual Behavior	Group, Organizational, and Political Behavior	Communication and Control	Organizational Design and Development	Connectedness	Dependency	System Dynamics	Emergence	Uncertainty	
ASSESSMENT QUESTIONS											
20	Does the organization have the right people, with the necessary skills and competencies, as well as the tools, techniques, or resources to support the program or project?										
21	Is the senior management team fully committed to the program or project?										
22	Will the program or project be conducted over a relatively short period of time, with a manageable number of stakeholder changes?										
23	Does the program or project have the support, commitment, and priority from the organization and functional groups?										
24	Is funding for the program or project being obtained from a single source or sponsor?										

(Continued)

Table X3-1. Mapping Template for Navigating Complexity (Continued)

Scenario Description:

Applicable Assessment Questions

Areas of Causes of Complexity ———>

Causes of Complexity ———>

Negative responses for questions:

ASSESSMENT QUESTIONS	No Responses	Human Behavior				System Behavior			Ambiguity	
		Individual Behavior	Group, Organizational, and Political Behavior	Communication and Control	Organizational Design and Development	Connectedness	Dependency	System Dynamics	Emergence	Uncertainty
25 Have the success criteria for the program or project been defined, documented, and agreed upon by stakeholders?										
26 For a multiorganizational-sponsored program or project, are all organizations aligned regarding project management processes, tools, and techniques?										
27 Are there a manageable number of third-party program or project relationships?										
28 Has this type of program or project ever been undertaken by the organization?										
29 Are the actual rate and type or propensity for change manageable?										
30 Does the program or project have a manageable number of issues, risks, and uncertainties?										

(Continued)

©2014 Project Management Institute. *Navigating Complexity: A Practice Guide*

Table X3-1. Mapping Template for Navigating Complexity *(Continued)*

Scenario Description:

			Human Behavior				System Behavior			Ambiguity	
	Applicable Assessment Questions ⟶										
	Causes of Complexity ⟶		Individual Behavior	Group, Organizational, and Political Behavior	Communication and Control	Organizational Design and Development	Connectedness	Dependency	System Dynamics	Emergence	Uncertainty
	ASSESSMENT QUESTIONS	No Responses									
31	Are the legal or regulatory requirements to which the program or project must comply manageable?										
32	Will suppliers be able to meet commitments to the program or project?										
33	Is there a high degree of confidence in the estimate to complete (ETC) for the program or project?										
34	Have realistic expectations been set around the business value that the program or project outcomes will produce?										
35	Will the program or project deliver to the committed deadlines?										
36	Is the client prepared to accept and sign off on the deliverables?										

Negative responses for questions:

(Continued)

Table X3-1. Mapping Template for Navigating Complexity *(Continued)*

Scenario Description:

			Human Behavior				System Behavior			Ambiguity	
	Negative responses for questions:		Individual Behavior	Group, Organizational, and Political Behavior	Communication and Control	Organizational Design and Development	Connectedness	Dependency	System Dynamics	Emergence	Uncertainty
Applicable Assessment Questions ——→											
Areas of Causes of Complexity ——→											
Causes of Complexity ——→	No Responses										
ASSESSMENT QUESTIONS											
37	Are the program or project documents and files being kept current in an accessible location for the team (e.g., plan baseline, final plan, change authorizations, payments, correspondence, or contracts)?										
38	Have all contracts related to the program or project been free from any claims filed by suppliers or customers?										
39	Have all parts of the program or project been free from any financial penalties?										
40	Is an agreed framework in place for financial tracking at a work package level?										
41	Are the program or project metrics appropriate, stable, and reported regularly?										

(Continued)

Table X3-1. Mapping Template for Navigating Complexity *(Continued)*

Scenario Description:

			Human Behavior				System Behavior			Ambiguity	
ASSESSMENT QUESTIONS	No Responses	Individual Behavior	Group, Organizational, and Political Behavior	Communication and Control	Organizational Design and Development	Connectedness	Dependency	System Dynamics	Emergence	Uncertainty
42	Is there a high level of confidence that new information generated from progressive elaboration are captured appropriately in the program or project plan?										
43	Is there a high level of confidence that the interconnected components of the program or project will perform in a predictable manner?										
44	Is it possible to terminate, suspend, or cancel a program or project activity when there is evidence that the achievement of the desired outcome is not possible?										
45	Are team members or stakeholders able to accept the program or project data or information that may be contrary to their beliefs, assumptions, or perspectives?										

Applicable Assessment Questions

Areas of Causes of Complexity ———→

Causes of Complexity ———→

Negative responses for questions:

(Continued)

Table X3-1. Mapping Template for Navigating Complexity *(Continued)*

Scenario Description:

			Human Behavior				System Behavior			Ambiguity	
ASSESSMENT QUESTIONS	No Responses	Individual Behavior	Group, Organizational, and Political Behavior	Communication and Control	Organizational Design and Development	Connectedness	Dependency	System Dynamics	Emergence	Uncertainty
46	Is there an effective portfolio management process within the organization to facilitate strategic alignment and enable successful delivery of programs and projects?										
47	Does the sponsor organization or project organization conduct its business (e.g., make decisions, determine strategies, set priorities, etc.) in a manner that promotes transparency and trust among its internal and external stakeholders?										
48	Are there a manageable number of critical paths in the program or project?										

Applicable Assessment Questions ——→
Areas of Causes of Complexity ——→
Causes of Complexity ——→
Negative responses for questions:

GLOSSARY

Adaptability. The ability to adapt to a changing environment and/or situation and to adopt a flexible approach that shifts according to the situation.

Ambiguity. A state of being unclear, of not knowing what to expect or how to comprehend a situation. It is one of the three categories of complexity identified in this practice guide.

Anchoring. A cognitive bias that causes people to fixate on an early piece of data even when contradicted by more accurate subsequent data.

Change Control. A process whereby modifications to documents, deliverables, or baselines associated with the project are identified, documented, approved, or rejected.

Component. An identifiable element within the program or project that provides a particular function or group of related functions.

Complexity. A characteristic of a program or project or its environment, which is difficult to manage due to human behavior, system behavior, and ambiguity.

Communications Method. A systematic procedure, technique, or process used to transfer information among project stakeholders.

Critical Thinking. A process in which one applies observation, analysis, inference, context, reflective thinking, and the like, in order to reach judgments. Such judgments should be open to alternative perspectives that may not normally be otherwise considered.

Emergent Complexity. The spontaneous, unanticipated change that occurs in a program or project and which acts as a major source of uncertainty.

Environmental Scan. A process that thoroughly reviews and interprets environmental data in order to develop SWOT analysis.

External Audits. These activities involve commissioning a team of objective experts to assess the validity of senior management expectations regarding program or project costs and benefits. These experts could be internal or external to the organization.

Feedback. A process in which the effect or output of an action is "returned" (fed back) to modify the next action.

Flat Organization. An organization in which many management levels between the highest and lowest levels have been minimized.

Framing Effect. A cognitive bias in which the manner that information is presented or an experiment is conducted irrationally affects the interpretation of data.

Governance. The framework for directing and enabling an organization through its established policies, practices, and other relevant documentation.

Groupthink. The phenomenon in which the group's desire to achieve conformity and harmony affects the rationality of its decisions.

Groupshift. The phenomenon in which the interactions among members of a group cause it to take more extreme positions than its members would normally take individually.

Holistic. Reviewing, relating, or treating entire systems and their environments, rather than separately reviewing or investigating the components of these systems.

Human Behavior. One of the three categories of complexity used in this practice guide to describe a source of complexity that occurs from the interplay of conducts, demeanors, and attitudes of people.

Interconnectedness. The interdependence of one individual, component, or objective on other individuals, components, or objectives in a program or project.

Interdependency. The state of mutual reliance between two or more entities, that is, the relationship in which each program or project component is mutually dependent on others. This characteristic differs from a dependence relationship, where some components are dependent and some are not.

Interdisciplinary Process Integration. The effective integration of processes from multiple disciplines.

Key Performance Indicator (KPI). A high-level measurement meant to indicate how well an individual or group is performing a set of activities that is considered critical to the overall success of an endeavor.

Leadership Skills. One of the three key skill sets that is considered as required for successful management of projects. Leadership skills include: negotiation, communication, motivation, problem solving, and related competencies.

Lessons Learned. The knowledge gained during a project, which shows how project events were addressed or should be addressed in the future for the purpose of improving future performance.

Loss Aversion. A cognitive bias in which people continue to support a clearly failing endeavor for which significant resources have already been expended. Also called sunk cost bias.

Misrepresentation. The deliberate presentation of false information in order to achieve personal gain.

NGO. Nongovernmental organization.

Oversimplification. Simplifying something to a point where its meaning is misrepresented or no longer accurate.

Overlooked Dependency. The potentially hidden connections among individual components in a hierarchical system.

Opacity. The unclear, secretive manner in which an organization conducts its business, such as making decisions, determining strategies, and setting priorities, which causes a lack of trust among stakeholders.

Part. A complete, integrated set of components and/or subsystems capable of accomplishing an operational role or function.

Planning Fallacy. The natural tendency of people to underestimate probable costs or time and to overestimate probable benefits of the required efforts to complete a task.

Paradoxical Thinking. The ability to hold two contradictory thoughts about a single issue (e.g., relaxing while sprinting, loosening control amidst instability).

Premortem Review. These are detailed reviews by experts to consider potential risks that could ultimately cause the failure of a program or project. Risk remediation effort estimates are added to original estimates to reset the budget, scope, and schedule expectations.

Portfolio. Projects, programs, subportfolios, and operations managed as a group to achieve strategic objectives.

Portfolio Management. The centralized management of one or more portfolios to achieve strategic objectives.

Program. A group of related projects, subprograms, and program activities that are managed in a coordinated way to obtain benefits not available from managing them individually.

Program Management. The application of knowledge, skills, tools, and techniques to a program to meet the program requirements and to obtain benefits and control not available by managing projects individually.

Program Manager. The individual within an agency, organization, or corporation who maintains responsibility for the leadership, conduct, and performance of a program.

Program Management Office. A management structure that standardizes the program-related governance processes and facilitates the sharing of resources, methodologies, tools, and techniques.

Project. A temporary endeavor undertaken to create a unique product, service, or result.

Project Life Cycle. The series of phases that a project passes through from its initiation to its closure.

Project Management. The application of knowledge, skills, tools, and techniques to project activities to meet the project requirements.

Project Management Office. An organizational structure that standardizes the project-related governance processes and facilitates the sharing of resources, methodologies, tools, and techniques.

Project Manager. The person assigned by the performing organization to lead the team that is responsible for achieving the project objectives.

RACI. A common type of responsibility assignment matrix that uses responsible, accountable, consult, and inform statuses to define the involvement of stakeholders in project activities.

Reference-Class Forecasting. A method for taking an outside view of preliminary program or project estimates in order to correct the mistakes brought on by cognitive biases.

Reflective Thinking. A part of the critical thinking process, the process of considering and elucidating one's self-experiences, which is best used to apply knowledge to future activities.

Requirement. A condition or capability that is required to be present in a product, service, or result to satisfy a contract or other formally imposed specification.

Resilience. The ability to cope with adversity and recover quickly from setbacks.

Resource Gap Analysis. An assessment comparing available resources with those needed for a program or project. The assessment may include reviewing areas such as resources, talent, software, alliances, processes, and practices readily available to successfully complete a program or project.

Risk. An uncertain event or condition that, if it occurs, has a positive or negative effect on one or more project objectives.

Scope. The work performed to deliver a project, service, or result with the specified features and functions.

Self-Organization. A spontaneous act where people come together and establish a structure or function in a purposeful manner.

Skills Assessment. A part of the resource gap analysis comparing available talents with those needed for a program or project.

Sponsor. A person or group who provides resources and support for the project, program, or portfolio and is accountable for enabling success.

Stakeholder. An individual, group, or organization who may affect, be affected by, or perceive itself to be affected by a decision, activity, or outcome of a project.

Stand-Up Meeting. A face-to-face meeting that is usually held in a location with no available chairs in order to facilitate a brief, focused meeting; however, the same outcome can be obtained by using the same technique and holding the meeting in a virtual environment.

Strategic and Business Management Skills. One of the three key skill sets that is considered as required for successful management of projects. Strategic and business management skills include: strategy alignment, innovation, finance, marketing, and operational functions, etc.

SWOT Analysis (Strengths, Weaknesses, Opportunities, and Threats). The analysis of strengths, weaknesses, opportunities, and threats of an organization, project, or option.

System. A collection of various components that together can produce results not obtainable by the components alone.

System Behavior. One of the three categories of complexity used in this practice guide to describe a source of complexity that may arise from the interactions and interdependence of various structures through connections among their parts or components.

System Dynamics. The interactions of connected and interdependent components, which may cause change over time and give rise to interconnected risks; emerging, unforeseeable issues; and unclear, disproportional cause-and-effect relationships.

Technical Project Management. One of the three key skill sets that is considered as required for successful management of projects. Technical project management skills include project management knowledge, product knowledge, and industry expertise.

Tribal Mindset. The "us vs. them" mentality that causes groups to take positions that ultimately thwart common goals and objectives.

Uncertainty. A lack of awareness and understanding of issues, events, path to follow, or solutions to pursue. Uncertainty may increase and amplify issues, risks, behaviors, or situations, which are internal and external to a program or project.

Unpredictability. Unpredictability is a common outcome of programs and projects in a complex environment. Social and political interactions and interconnectedness can create issues and/or results that are unable to be predetermined.

INDEX